Social Studies Plus!
A Hands-On Approach

Editorial Offices: Glenview, Illinois • Parsippany, New Jersey • New York, New York
Sales Offices: Parsippany, New Jersey • Duluth, Georgia • Glenview, Illinois •
Coppell, Texas • Ontario, California

www.sfsocialstudies.com

Program Authors

Dr. Candy Dawson Boyd
Professor, School of Education
Director of Reading Programs
St. Mary's College
Moraga, California

Dr. Geneva Gay
Professor of Education
University of Washington
Seattle, Washington

Rita Geiger
Director of Social Studies and
    Foreign Languages
Norman Public Schools
Norman, Oklahoma

Dr. James B. Kracht
Associate Dean for
    Undergraduate Programs
    and Teacher Education
College of Education
Texas A&M University
College Station, Texas

Dr. Valerie Ooka Pang
Professor of Teacher Education
San Diego State University
San Diego, California

Dr. C. Frederick Risinger
Director, Professional
    Development and Social
    Studies Education
Indiana University
Bloomington, Indiana

Sara Miranda Sanchez
Elementary and Early
    Childhood Curriculum
    Coordinator
Albuquerque Public Schools
Albuquerque, New Mexico

Contributing Authors

Dr. Carol Berkin
Professor of History
Baruch College and the
    Graduate Center
The City University of New York
New York, New York

Lee A. Chase
Staff Development Specialist
Chesterfield County
    Public Schools
Chesterfield County, Virginia

Dr. Jim Cummins
Professor of Curriculum
Ontario Institute for Studies
    in Education
University of Toronto
Toronto, Canada

Dr. Allen D. Glenn
Professor and Dean Emeritus
Curriculum and Instruction
College of Education
University of Washington
Seattle, Washington

Dr. Carole L. Hahn
Professor, Educational Studies
Emory University
Atlanta, Georgia

Dr. M. Gail Hickey
Professor of Education
Indiana University-Purdue
    University
Fort Wayne, Indiana

Dr. Bonnie Meszaros
Associate Director
Center for Economic Education
    and Entrepreneurship
University of Delaware
Newark, Delaware

ISBN: 0-328-03592-0

6 7 8 9 10 V016 09 08 07 06 05 04

Contents

Welcome to *Social Studies Plus!*

Using Activities to Launch Social Studies Classes

Most educators are all too familiar with the "banking" metaphor of learning, where students sit passively as receivers of information. Educators also know the need to switch that construct to a vital one where students *participate* in the wide world that social studies class can reveal. To jump-start this new metaphor, it helps to have a variety of dynamic and broad-range activities that draw life and direction from the content and skills of basic social studies curriculum. In this way, students begin to realize that the issues of social studies concern things they care about.

Social studies, of course, is about both the forest and the trees. It covers the whole world—big and little events, heroes and ordinary people, issues of justice, morality, and ethics. Social studies is also about the *specific*—the content and skills connected with historical fact and assessing controversial issues that students learn to work with at their own levels of understanding.

When we teach social studies, it is important to join all the important historical, political, and economic aspects of the curriculum with the concrete ways students learn and express themselves. It makes sense, then, to engage students in many different kinds of activities so as to appeal to the varied ways students tackle any curriculum but especially the broad curriculum of social studies. A variety of approaches helps students internalize what citizenship means and how important participation is for a democracy to thrive.

Social Studies Plus! Overview and Purpose

Social Studies Plus! begins with Scott Foresman's social studies basal scope and sequence and then sets up engaging activities that invite students to think independently about events and issues in both the past and present. Some activities create a storytelling atmosphere, where students can move from the concrete to the abstract. Some *Social Studies Plus!* activities

place the student in the middle of an historical event and ask the student to take a position and justify it. Other activities promote discussion, questioning, and analysis about the consequences resulting from events, ideas, and persons' actions. Not only should the ideas presented open students' thinking and get them interested in social studies curriculum, the activities should also help students see that they have something at stake in the issues of being a citizen.

Social Studies Plus! offers several approaches in which students may participate:

- Students may create simulations by playing various roles; for instance, they may become members of an immigrant family arriving at Ellis Island, or they may act out the parts of weary soldiers at Valley Forge under General George Washington.

- Students may dig into hands-on activities by drawing themselves on "living" time lines as characters in the early colonies or on the Underground Railroad.

- Students may use their math and graphic organizer skills to map out or graph the fast clip of progress during the Industrial Revolution.

- Students may design labor union broadsides or cartoons about the 1920s, which then may trigger critical discussions of moral and ethical issues.

- Some students may use biographical sketches of famous people in history to stimulate their own writing of persuasive speeches, poems, or news articles that show a variety of perspectives.

Each unit follows a basic progression. First, a Long-Term Project presents a unit theme for students to work on throughout the study of the unit. Second, other unit themes are presented in creative and dramatic form in a six-page Drama section. Third, a number of Short-Term Projects, Writing Projects, and Citizenship activities further develop the topics covered in each chapter.

Read ahead to see how each unit is mapped out and how to make the most of all the projects and activities presented in *Social Studies Plus!*

Unit Development

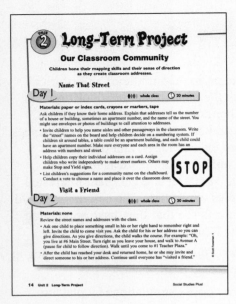

Long-Term Project

Students are offered a Long-Term Project that may last several days or weeks. The goal of the project is to extend the main ideas of an entire unit and allow students enough time to perform one or several tasks. For instance, students may draw, make graphs, do an interview, or complete some research on one topic. With the Long-Term Project, students have time to enter into the discussion of an issue, or they launch into making something concrete, such as a model, diorama, puppets, and so on. The unit project, then, allows students to integrate key social studies concepts and skills in an organized, and often artistic, way.

These unit-sized projects may suggest that the teacher set the context or recall topics at hand, or the teacher may choose how much background to give students. Students do not always need prior experience with the topics presented. Procedures for handling the project are laid out in easy-to-follow steps where teachers may choose the grouping and specific tasks so that, by unit's end, everyone contributes to an overall display or project. Students usually end up choosing what goes into a report or display, allowing them the chance to *own* a part of the display. One of the most enlightening parts of the unit project happens when students present their endeavors to one another or to other classes. A close second to that experience occurs when their audiences ask the students questions and the students become experts for the moment.

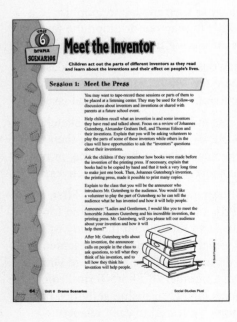

Drama: Plays

Every activity in the Drama section of *Social Studies Plus!* is aimed at creating a dramatic and physical reaction in students to some social studies issues. All the activities give students opportunities for improvising.

The plays are presented either as fully written scripts or as plays with some written lines and suggested ways for improvising additional lines and scenes. In addition, most plays are based on the following parameters:

- The plays take no longer than 30–40 minutes at a time, although play practice and presentation may extend over several class periods.

- The plays are appropriate for each age group in both dialogue and plot complexity.

- The plays are accompanied by a director's guide that will help the student-leader or teacher by providing plot summary, prop and theater term suggestions, or character descriptions.

Drama: Scenarios

Scenarios give students the opportunity to act out brief scenes that draw on their spur-of-the-moment reactions as well as promote their abilities to think on their feet. These scenarios relate to the topics and skills at hand and do not require outside research. Each scenario will:

- provide students with a purpose and focus for the scenario,

- often suggest a conflict relevant to the students' life experiences,

- be easily done in the classroom with a few optional props,

- take only about 10–15 minutes to present,

- and often allow students opportunities to think beyond their usual perspective about facts and people.

Chapter Development

Short-Term Projects

The goal of the many Short-Term Projects is to extend the chapter content. No projects are repeated from the Teacher's Edition. Rather they proceed from the themes and topics of interest in the Student's Edition and so allow students a myriad of hands-on activities. These projects are oriented toward engaging students in the following ways:

- Short-Term Projects engage small groups, partners, individuals or the whole class in relevant activities.

- They encompass a wide variety of activities: map making, debates, theme mobiles, banners and collages, speeches, time lines from Ancient Egypt to the town of Egypt, Maine, and many more.

- They suggest ways for the students to have fun with social studies topics and skills.

- They cover skills to help students think "out of the box."

- They offer directions that students may follow without much adult assistance.

- They integrate various subject areas into a social studies project.

- They can be completed in about 20–30 minutes.

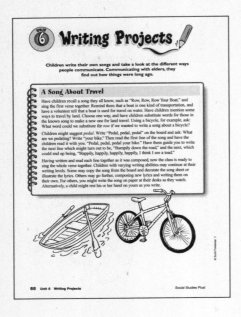

Writing Projects

In a grab bag approach, some Writing Projects allow a wide swath of creativity and some take students through brief, but rigorous, expository writing. The Writing Projects should also include the following goals.

- The Writing Projects engage students in a variety of dynamic writing applications of social studies content and skills and can be completed in about 20–30 minutes.

- They serve as a bridge between students' (a) prior knowledge and life experiences and (b) content of the core text.

- They provide a connection between concrete/operational understanding and the application of social studies concepts/skills to a student's life.

- They should help students experience social studies in ways other than rehashing dates and events.

- They should be intriguing enough to make teachers and students *both* want to try the activities.

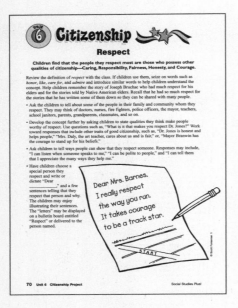

Citizenship

Social studies always deals with citizens of the past and present. To show students how important participation is in a democratic society, these activities focus on the traits of a good citizen.

- Each Citizenship page may require some research, creative writing, interviews, or artistic endeavors.

- The goal of this page is to make students more aware of how to spot citizenship traits in their own actions and in the larger neighborhood or community around them.

Blackline Masters

Each chapter has at least one blackline master for students to use to further extend one or more of the activities in the unit or chapter. Some of these pages engage students in crossword puzzles, cartoon strips and storyboards, graphic organizers, map and graph making, and various kinds of artwork.

Assessment for *Social Studies Plus!*

The rubrics suggested for use with *Social Studies Plus!* materials are intended to aid teachers in recording a range of the students' linguistic and cultural experiences.

The emphasis of these rubrics is placed on thinking rather than rote learning, performance and successes rather than failings, and on each individual's development within grade-level expectations. Obviously no rubrics are a substitute for the teacher's classroom observations. A teacher's notes on students' abilities to gain knowledge based on experience is key in helping teachers make students understand what they need to learn.

The rubrics presented in *Social Studies Plus!* pertain to assessing students' achievements while they are engaged in exploring the social studies content and learning new skills. Applying these rubrics to the students' work gives them concrete feedback and helps them monitor their own progress toward meeting performance standards. These rubrics are oriented toward assessing the variety of ways students may approach the content and skills of this program.

Writing Rubrics

Writing, because it is specific and tangible, may be easier to evaluate than most other subjects. Both analytic and holistic rubrics are used to evaluate writing. Many teachers use holistic scoring because it evaluates a writer's overall ability to express meaning in written form.

Analytic rubrics tend to incorporate spelling, punctuation, and grammar accuracy, yet they also address some complex aspects of writing assessment. This rubric is based on the assumption that teachers will be looking at students' abilities to begin handling some stages of the writing process in relation to social studies content. Once students have some specific ideas of how to improve their writing, they can begin to be their own editors.

4-point rubric

4 Excellent **3** Very Good **2** Satisfactory **1** Needs Improvement

Six Traits for the Analytic Writing Rubric

Content Quality and Idea Development

control of topic, interesting, clear, ideas developed, organized, most details in place

Voice

specific, honest, engaging, a clear point of view, easy to follow

Organization

complete text, most details in place, some transitions, contains beginning, middle, and end

Word Precision

interesting word choice, appropriate use of action verbs

Sentence Fluency

some variation in sentence structure

Mechanics

handles simple grammar, sensible paragraphing, correct use of some punctuation, easy to read

Rubric for Narrative Writing

	4 Excellent	3 Very Good	2 Satisfactory	1 Needs Improvement
Content Quality and Idea Development	• well-developed story • well-focused on the topic • clear ideas	• fairly well-developed story • focused on the topic	• sometimes strays from topic • ideas are not well-developed	• poorly focused on the topic • ideas are unclear
Voice	• voice is fitting for the topic and engaging	• voice is fairly clear and seems to fit the topic	• voice rarely comes through	• voice is weak or inappropriate
Organization	• well-focused on the topic • logical organization • sequence is very clear	• generally focused on the topic • some lapses in organization • has a beginning, middle, and end	• somewhat focused on the topic • poor organization and some difficulty with sequence	• not focused on the topic • no clear organization • no clear sequence
Word Precision	• precise, vivid, and interesting word choices • variety of word choices	• fairly precise, interesting, and somewhat varied word choices	• vague, mundane word choices • wording is repetitive	• very limited word choices • wording is bland
Sentence Fluency	• uses complete sentences • varying sentence structures	• uses complete sentences • generally simple sentence structures	• occasional sentence fragment or run-on sentence • simple sentence structure is used repeatedly	• frequent use of sentence fragments or run-on sentences • sentences are difficult to understand
Mechanics	• proper grammar and usage • correct spelling • correct punctuation	• few errors of grammar and usage • mostly correct spelling	• errors in grammar, usage, and spelling	• frequent errors in grammar, usage, and spelling make understanding difficult

Rubric for Persuasive Writing

	4 Excellent	3 Very Good	2 Satisfactory	1 Needs Improvement
Content Quality and Idea Development	• clear position is well-supported • complete control of topic • many facts and opinions	• clear position is somewhat supported • good control of topic • some facts and opinions	• position is taken, but not supported • some control of topic • few facts and opinions	• no clear position taken • little control of topic • no facts and opinions given
Voice	• voice is strong and engaging • specific, honest point of view • well-suited for audience and purpose	• voice is fairly strong • generally clear point of view • suited for audience and purpose	• voice rarely comes through • general, vague discussion of topic • not always suited for audience and purpose	• voice is weak or inappropriate • no particular point of view presented • no sense of audience or purpose
Organization	• well-focused on the topic • logical organization • contains beginning, middle, and end • easy to follow	• generally focused on the topic • organization is mostly clear • contains beginning, middle, and end • usually easy to follow	• somewhat focused on the topic • poor organization • no clear beginning, middle, and end • difficult to follow	• not focused on the topic • no clear organization • no clear beginning, middle, and end
Word Precision	• precise, persuasive word choices • fluency of thought • appropriate use of action verbs	• fairly precise, persuasive word choices • generally appropriate use of action verbs	• vague, unpersuasive word choices • wording is sometimes repetitive	• very limited word choices • fails to persuade • wording is redundant and bland
Sentence Fluency	• uses complete sentences • varying sentence structures	• uses complete sentences • generally simple sentence structures	• occasional sentence fragment • simple sentence structure is used repeatedly	• frequent use of sentence fragments • sentences are difficult to understand
Mechanics	• proper grammar and usage • correct spelling • correct punctuation	• few errors of grammar and usage • mostly correct spelling and punctuation	• errors in grammar, usage, and spelling • some errors in punctuation	• frequent errors in grammar, usage, and spelling make understanding difficult

Rubric for Expressive/Descriptive Writing

	4 Excellent	3 Very Good	2 Satisfactory	1 Needs Improvement
Content Quality and Idea Development	• "paints a picture" for the reader • well-focused on the topic • clear ideas and vivid details	• creates some clear images for the reader • focused on the topic • some details	• sometimes strays from topic • ideas are not well-developed • needs more details	• poorly focused on the topic • ideas are unclear • few details are given
Voice	• voice is fitting for the topic • well-suited for audience and purpose	• voice is fairly clear • suited for audience and purpose	• voice rarely comes through • not always suited for audience and purpose	• voice is weak or inappropriate • no sense of audience or purpose
Organization	• well focused on the topic • logical organization • excellent transitions • easy to follow	• generally focused on the topic • some lapses in organization • some transitions • usually easy to follow	• somewhat focused on the topic • poor organization • few transitions • difficult to follow	• not focused on the topic • no clear organization • no transitions • difficult to impossible to follow
Word Precision	• vivid and interesting word choices • a variety of word choices	• interesting word choices • wording could be more specific	• vague, mundane word choices • wording is repetitive	• very limited word choices • wording is bland and not descriptive
Sentence Fluency	• uses complete sentences • varying sentence structures	• uses complete sentences • generally simple sentence structures	• occasional sentence fragment or run-on sentence • simple sentence structure is used repeatedly	• frequent use of sentence fragments or run-on sentences • sentences are difficult to understand
Mechanics	• proper grammar and usage • correct spelling • correct punctuation	• few errors of grammar and usage • mostly correct spelling and punctuation	• errors in grammar and usage make understanding difficult • some errors in punctuation	• frequent errors in grammar and usage make understanding difficult or impossible

Rubric for Expository Writing

	4 Excellent	3 Very Good	2 Satisfactory	1 Needs Improvement
Content Quality and Idea Development	• well-focused on the topic • clear ideas with interesting details	• focused on the topic • ideas with details	• sometimes strays from topic • ideas are not well-developed	• poorly focused on the topic • ideas are unclear
Voice	• voice is strong • well-suited for audience and purpose	• voice is fairly strong • suited for audience and purpose	• voice rarely comes through • not always suited for audience and purpose	• voice is weak or inappropriate • no sense of audience or purpose
Organization	• well-focused on the topic • logical organization • excellent transitions • easy to follow	• generally focused on the topic • organization is mostly clear • some transitions • usually easy to follow	• somewhat focused on the topic • poor organization • few transitions • difficult to follow	• not focused on the topic • no clear organization • no transitions • difficult to impossible to follow
Word Precision	• interesting word choices • variety of word choices	• fairly interesting word choices • wording could be more specific	• vague, mundane word choices • wording is repetitive	• very limited word choices • wording is bland
Sentence Fluency	• strong topic sentence • varying sentence structures • uses complete sentences	• good topic sentence • generally simple sentence structures • some complete sentences	• weak topic sentence • simple sentence structure is used repeatedly • occasional sentence fragment	• no topic sentence • sentences are difficult to understand • frequent use of sentence fragments
Mechanics	• proper grammar and usage • correct spelling • correct punctuation	• few errors of grammar and usage • mostly correct spelling and punctuation	• errors in grammar and usage	• frequent errors in grammar and usage make understanding difficult or impossible

Class Projects Rubric

Social Studies Plus! presents numerous projects, for both individual and group work, making the rubric for the elements of content and skill more general. Many of the students' products resulting from these projects may be assessed as well by placing some in student portfolios or displaying them in the classroom. The rubric below is a general guide for assessing the projects.

Individual/Collaborative Projects

Directions: Copy the rubric for either groups or individuals. Circle the appropriate number for individual and collaborative participation in the projects.

Skill/Performance	Excellent	Very Good	Satisfactory	Needs Improvement
1. Collaborative reading/ understand task	4	3	2	1
2. Group listens to group leader	4	3	2	1
3. Group members listen to one another	4	3	2	1
4. Group understands cross-curricular skills needed	4	3	2	1
5. Group designs and constructs project in organized way	4	3	2	1
6. Individual uses right skills for environmental and historical research	4	3	2	1
7. Individual plans and executes art/craft project	4	3	2	1
8. Individual uses prior knowledge to complete task	4	3	2	1
9. Individual uses skill strategies, such as comparison, analysis, outlining, and map reading to complete task	4	3	2	1
10. Individual shows ability to reflect on what is the topic and what is important	4	3	2	1

Drama Rubric

Directions: Make a form for each student. Circle the appropriate number for each individual's participation in the play or scenario.

Student Name: _____

Skill/Performance	Excellent	Very Good	Satisfactory	Needs Improvement
1. Understands task	4	3	2	1
2. Plans own part	4	3	2	1
3. Understands the movement in front of group; maintains eye contact	4	3	2	1
4. Researched and practiced part	4	3	2	1
5. Willing to improvise in context	4	3	2	1
6. Projection and diction	4	3	2	1
7. Concentration and poise in acting	4	3	2	1
8. Language clear and delivered with enthusiasm	4	3	2	1
9. Understood content correctly	4	3	2	1
10. Delivered in believable way	4	3	2	1

Long-Term Project pages 2–3	Materials	🕐	Lesson Link
We Are Special Students have a flag waving celebration.			Lessons 1–4
Day 1 👥 **whole class** Students discuss the special groups they belong to.	chalkboard or chart paper	1 session 15 min.	
Day 2 👥 **whole class** Students write those groups down on strips of paper.	strips of paper (1" x 5"), pencils, tape	1 session 15 min.	
Day 3 👥 **whole class** Students design a symbol for one of the groups.	school's logo, drawing paper, crayons	1 session 40 min.	
Day 4 👥 **whole class** Students attach their symbols to paper flags.	children's symbols, various art supplies	1 session 15 min.	
Day 5 👥 **whole class** Students hold a flag ceremony, and display their flags on a bulletin board.	children's flags, charts with groups' names	1 session 15 min.	
Unit Drama pages 4–5			
Scenarios: We Can Solve It 👥 **group** Students role-play skits about the problems that may arise when we work and play in groups.	BLM p. 11	3 sessions 25 min. each	Lesson 2
Short-Term Projects pages 6–7			
Hidden Pictures 🧍 **individual** Students illustrate an area of their school that most interests them.	paper, crayons, oaktag, scissors	1 session 20 min.	Lesson 4
Every Day is Special! 👥 **whole class** Students draw pictures of one thing that makes that day special for them.	paper, crayons or markers	1 session 20 min.	Lesson 2
A Classroom Tour! 👥 **whole class** Students organize a tour of the classroom to show others what goes on during the day.	paper, crayons or markers	1 session 20 min.	Lesson 4
Writing Projects pages 8–9			
Lunchtime Joy 🧍 **individual** Students write or draw a menu for lunch in the cafeteria.	paper, pencils, crayons	1 session 25 min.	Lesson 1
The Cafeteria Rules 🧍 **individual** Students write letters to the cafeteria staff thanking them for their help in making lunch an enjoyable time.	paper, pencils, letter templates	1 session 25 min.	Lesson 3
How Did That Happen? 🧍 **individual** Students make up sentences about a picture to tell what happened.	BLM p. 12, paper, pencils, crayons	1 session 30 min.	Lesson 4
Citizenship Project page 10			
Courage 👥 **whole class** Students make a chart and drawing about needing courage in different situations.	paper, pencils, chalkboard, crayons	1 session 40 min.	Lessons 1–2

Long-Term Project

We Are Special

Let's have a flag waving celebration for our groups! Children will discover that they are special members of many different groups.

Meet Our Special Groups

Day 1

 whole class   15 minutes

Materials: chalkboard or chart paper

Begin by asking children if they, siblings, or friends participate in sports. If so, they are members of a team or a special kind of group. Discuss how people often learn, work, and play in groups. Ask the children to name groups they belong to such as scouts.

- Make a column for each type of group to which the children belong. For example, the category "Sports Teams" may include soccer or T-ball. Leave space under each group to add members' names at a later session.

- Explain that we are all members of a family, which is a special group. Classes, schools, communities, and countries are also groups. Write these groups on the list.

- Quickly review all of the groups. Explain that some are members of some groups and others are members of other groups. Sometimes classmates all belong to the same group.

We Are Part of Many Groups

Day 2

 whole class   15 minutes

Materials: 5 strips of paper per child (1"x 5"), pencils, and tape

- Distribute 5 strips of paper to each child and ask them to print their name on each strip. Review the groups on your chart one by one, assign a child to each group to call out the group name, then ask children to raise their hand if they belong to a group. Assist children in taping name strips under the correct group.

- Check to see that all children have membership in at least five groups. If not, ask the children if there are any groups to add. Help them think of other groups, write these new categories on the chart, and add children's names. Allow children an opportunity to stand and name the groups to which they belong.

Day 3
Symbols for Our Groups

👤👤👤 whole class   🕐 40 minutes

Materials: the school's logo, drawing paper cut in rectangles, crayons

Lead children in a discussion about our flag as a symbol for our country. Explain that there are 50 stars—one for each state, and 13 stripes—one for each of the original colonies. If your school has a logo, display it for all to see. Discuss how it represents the group called "Our School." Explain that a group they all belong to is "Our Class." Ask: What makes your class special? Brainstorm possible symbols for your class.

Put children into groups of 3 or 4 to design a symbol for one of the groups from Day 2. Ask them to decide the symbol, pick someone to draw the symbol, color the symbol, and copy the name of the group on the back of their paper. Distribute the paper and drawing tools and then collect the completed symbols for the next session.

Day 4
Making a Flag

👤👤👤 whole class   🕐 15 minutes

Materials: children's symbols from the previous day, colored paper, glue, black marker, unsharpened pencils or cardboard strips for flag pole and tape.

Invite volunteers to share their group's symbol with the class and tell why they chose their symbol. Assist the children in gluing the symbol on colored paper flags and in taping or gluing their flag to a pencil or cardboard strip flagpole.

Day 5
Flag Waving Ceremony

👤👤👤 whole class   🕐 15 minutes

Materials: children's flags and the charts with groups and members' names

Gather the children in a large circle on the floor. Tell them when you raise a flag, all the members of that group may stand in the middle of the circle to be recognized. Give the flag to a group member to wave and pass to each member to wave. Clap for each group.

You may want to invite another class to your ceremony, plan a parade around your classroom, display the flags on a bulletin board.

We Can Solve It

**When we work and play in groups, problems sometimes arise.
See a problem? You can solve it! Learn the tools in 6 easy steps**

Session 1: Learning the Steps

Write the six Problem-Solving Steps on the board. Tell your class a story like the one that follows about children who choose sides for playing a game.

"Once there was a First Grade Class very much like ours who wanted to play a game called 'Relay Race.' This race needed to have the same number on each team. The first runner on each team had a building block in one hand. After running to the chalkboard and back, the first runner would hand the block to the next player until everyone ran once. The teacher was the starter. She was all ready to say, 'Go,' when a child noticed that one line was longer than the other. The children counted the number on each team. Guess what? Team A had one more runner than Team B. That wouldn't be fair because the first team to finish won the race. How could the class solve this problem?"

• Pass out copies of the Problem Solving Steps Blackline Master on page 11 and have children track with their finger each step as you read it from the board. Read Step 1 aloud and encourage the children to state the problem in their own words. Repeat the procedure for Step 2, exploring the problem further.

• Choose 7 volunteers to line up to play the roles of Team A and Team B while the rest of the class becomes the audience. Call one child on Team B aside privately and ask him or her to be the one who notices the other team has more members. You can play the teacher's role.

• When a child discovers the problem, ask: What in the world are we going to do now?

• Put the question to both teams and to the audience. List all the recommendations next to Step 3 on the board. "Now, which one of these ideas is the best way to solve the problem? Next time we work on this problem, we'll pick the best way and have our teams act out our solution."

Session 2: Choose the Best Solution

- Review the problem and read the suggested solutions aloud. Help children discuss the strengths and weaknesses of each. Then have each child draw a picture of his or her choice for the best solution.

- Have children vote for their choice and record the votes on the board. Draw a circle around the solution that has been chosen.

- Choose new players to be Team A and Team B. Help the teams act out the new solution. When the actors are finished, have them take seats facing the audience.

- Conduct a dialogue between actors and audience about how well the chosen solution worked, how it felt to be the extra person, and whether everyone on Team A and Team B felt the solution was fair.

PROBLEM	POSSIBLE SOLUTIONS
Too many children on Team A.	**Let the extra person be the starter.**
	Let the teacher be on Team B.
	Play a different game.

Session 3: More Solutions

Now that the class has some experience simulating problems and solutions, they can follow the procedures used in Session 2 to act out other solutions from their list, then analyze and compare the various solutions to the one they chose at the beginning. Be sure every child has the opportunity to participate.

Be alert to non-behavioral problems that occur in your classroom and on the playground. Take the problem to the class for them to solve. Display a copy of the Problem-Solving Steps Blackline Master and direct children to follow those steps in resolving the real-life situations.

Short-Term Projects

Rally around! It's time to show pride in our classroom and school. Try some of these activities so children will know ways their school and their class can be the best.

Hidden Pictures

 individual   20 minutes

Materials: paper, crayons or markers for each child, cover stock, tag board or other lightweight cardboard and scissors for the teacher

Prepare a cardboard shield by cutting out one corner (about $\frac{1}{4}$ of the whole piece) of an $8\frac{1}{2}$" by 11" piece of cardboard to fit over children's drawings.

• Discuss areas that make your classroom a special place to work and play such as the writing, reading and math corners. Expand the discussion to other parts of the school such as the cafeteria and library.

• Have children choose and illustrate one of the areas that most interests them. Remind children to let their drawing fill the page. When they have finished, collect their pictures.

• Using your template to cover one drawing at a time, have the children describe the part that can be seen and guess what the whole picture is about. Flip the template vertically or horizontally and have the children describe what they see and guess again. Continue flipping until the whole picture has been revealed in parts.

• Variations: (1) After modeling this procedure for the whole class, place the template and the stack of pictures at a center and have pairs of children take turns masking the pictures and guessing the whole from the part revealed. (2) Instead of children's drawings use photos from magazines.

Every Day is Special!

 whole class ⏱ **20 minutes**

Materials: paper, crayons or markers

When every day is a little different, the week is much more fun!

• Draw a chart on the board or on chart paper with 5 columns, each headed with a day of the week. Invite the children to read the days with you and remember the many things they do every day at school. List their ideas. Children may offer events such as, "On Mondays our class gets to use the computer lab." Provide hints for each day.

• Ask children to choose a day and draw a picture of one thing that makes that day special for them. Invite children to share and have classmates guess the day and the event. The pictures could be displayed on a bulletin board entitled "What Makes Every Day A Special Day At (school's name)."

...DAY	TUESDAY	WEDN...

A Classroom Tour!

 whole class ⏱ **20 minutes**

Materials: paper, crayons or markers

Explain to the children that sometimes visitors come to school to see what goes on in your classroom. A guided tour might be helpful to visitors. Ask if anyone has been on a guided tour of a museum or historic place. If so, invite them to explain what a guide does.

Ask a volunteer to be a tour guide and ask 4 or 5 other children to be the visitors. Ask the guide to start in an area of the room, explain what happens in the area, what the rules are, and who uses the space. Encourage children to ask questions a visitor might ask. Repeat the tour to allow all children to participate. (This may be carried out over several days.)

• After the tours, discuss what else could be done to make the tour more informative. Children may want to make a guest book with a place for guests' signatures and comments, or a classroom video.

• Invite the principal or some parents in for the grand tour. You may want to have each child give their parents a tour on Back to School Night or at parent/teacher conferences.

**Remember!
Keep working
on that
Long-Term Project.**

Unit 1 Writing Projects

What's the best school lunch of all? Find out from the children as they invent menus for their own lunches and make suggestions for a pleasant lunchtime experience.

Lunchtime Joy

Guide the class in a discussion about eating lunch at school. Some children bring their lunches and others eat lunch prepared by the school. Talk with children about foods they like. "What foods are good for us?" Discuss and list the major food groups and record some of their suggestions on the chalkboard under each of these groups.

Explain that the manager of the cafeteria and/or the children's parents might want to know their ideas about a good lunch menu. Invite them to write or draw a menu with the ideas the class has already suggested. Ask children to choose at least one food item from each food group. Suggest they make menu borders.

Tuna Salad on Whole Wheat Bread

Lettuce and Tomato

Little Carrots

Raisins

Milk

Granola Bar

The Cafeteria Rules

Ask children to discuss good table manners. List these on the chalkboard. Ask children what they think makes a good place to eat. What rules do we have that make our lunchroom a pleasant place to eat our lunches? What could we do to make sure everyone remembers those rules? What do the cafeteria manager, workers, and principal do that help to make lunch pleasurable? Suggest that the class writes a letter to the cafeteria manager, the cafeteria workers, and/or the principal thanking them for their help in making lunch an enjoyable time. Ask the class to explain in the letter what they think makes a good place to eat and what they think they can do to help everyone remember the rules.

(Date)_____

Dear (Cafeteria Manager or Principal),

We want to thank you for _____.

For lunch to be enjoyable for everyone, we think that children should _____.

Some additional ideas we have are _____ (list suggestions).

Sincerely yours,

The First Graders in Room _____

Have the class choose representatives to deliver it to the cafeteria manager, principal or other appropriate school staff person.

How Did It Happen?

Something went wrong in the kitchen! Children study a picture and make up sentences to tell what happened and how it happened!

Hand out a copy of the How Did It Happen? blackline master on page 12 to each child. Discuss the picture with the class. Ask children to describe what they see and write or dictate a sentence about what is happening in the picture without telling how they think it happened. Then have children decide how they think the scene happened and on a fresh piece of paper draw a picture showing how it happened. Under the picture they should write or dictate a story about how the milk got spilled.

Courage

What is courage? Firefighters need courage to help rescue people from burning buildings. Children need courage, too. We all need courage, even when we are working and playing in safe groups.

Tell children that some jobs that groups of people do are dangerous and require courage. For example, firefighters need courage to go into burning buildings to save people. Police men and women need courage to try to stop someone from hurting others.

There are other dangerous jobs people do that require courage. To do these jobs people must have special training and have special tools to be safe. Even with training and tools, they may feel afraid. When we are in danger it takes courage to be brave. (Make certain that children understand that untrained people should not attempt these dangerous jobs.)

Sometimes it takes courage to do things that aren't dangerous. It takes courage to stand up in front of the whole class to talk or perform.

It takes courage to learn something you don't know how to do, like learning to read. It takes courage to tell people that you don't like how they treat you. It also takes courage to tell someone that they look nice. It takes courage to talk to people we don't know well. Ask the class to discuss when they have needed courage at school. Write their ideas on the board.

Ask children how they learned to have courage to meet challenges such as these. You may want to begin by telling how you gather the courage to do something hard. Make a chart "Calling Up Courage" listing things we can do to help us find courage. Invite children to make a drawing about needing courage even in safe places like our school.

For Courage
at School
and on the Job!

Problem Solving Steps

Step 1   Name the problem.

Step 2   Find out more about the problem.

Step 3   List ways to solve the problem.

Step 4   Talk about the best way to solve the problem.

Step 5   Solve the problem.

Step 6   How well is the problem solved?

How Did It Happen?

Reason 1 _____

_____

Reason 2 _____

_____

Reason 3 _____

_____

Reason 4 _____

_____

Teacher Planner

Long-Term Project pages 14–15	Materials	🕐	Lesson Link
Our Classroom Community Students create classroom addresses.			Lesson 1
Day 1 🧍🧍🧍 **whole class** Students name aisles and passageways in the classroom.	paper or index cards, crayons or markers, tape	1 session 20 min.	
Day 2 🧍🧍🧍 **whole class** Students give directions to one another's desks.	none	1 session 20 min.	
Day 3 🧍🧍🧍 **whole class** Students make a map of their classroom.	paper, pencils or markers	1 session 15 min.	
Day 4 🧍🧍🧍 **whole class** Students locate their own addresses on the map.	maps from Day 3	1 session 15 min.	
Day 5 🧍🧍🧍 **whole class** Students make a chart comparing two communities.	paper, pencils or markers	1 session 15 min.	
Unit Drama pages 16–17			
Scenarios: Three House Builders and One Neighborhood Helper 🧍🧍🧍 **group** Students role-play a new version of "The Three Little Pigs."	homemade pig ears and wolf ears, BLM p. 23	3 sessions 25 min. each	Lesson 2
Short-Term Projects pages 18–19			
A Real SQUARE Dance 🧍🧍🧍 **whole class** Students follow square dance directions while practicing their direction skills.	directional signs, square dance music (optional)	1 session 45 min.	Lesson 3
Communities Large and Small 🧍🧍🧍 **whole class** Students create a list of books that are like their community and illustrate items from the list.	books, paper, pencils, crayons or markers	1 session 30 min.	Lesson 2
Writing Projects pages 20–21			
Special Places in Our Community 🧍 **individual** Students draw pictures and descriptions of places in the community that are special to them.	oaktag or index cards, pencils, crayons, BLM p. 24	1 session 30 min.	Lesson 3
Groups in Our Community 🧍 **individual** Students write sentences about a community group.	paper, pencils, crayons	1 session 20 min.	Lesson 4
Community Leaders 🧍 **individual** Students write letters asking a community leader to visit their class.	paper, pencils	1 session 25 min.	Lesson 4
Changes, Changes 🧍 **individual** Students write descriptions of a change in their community.	paper, pencils, crayons	1 session 20 min.	Lesson 5
Citizenship Project page 22			
Fairness 🧍🧍🧍 **whole class** Students illustrate situations showing fairness, and write sentences about what made the action fair.	paper, pencils, crayons	1 session 45 min.	Lessons 1–5

Long-Term Project

Our Classroom Community

Children hone their mapping skills and their sense of direction as they create classroom addresses.

Name That Street

Day 1

 whole class 20 minutes

Materials: paper or index cards, crayons or markers, tape

Ask children if they know their home address. Explain that addresses tell us the number of a house or building, sometimes an apartment number, and the name of the street. You might use envelopes or photos of buildings to call attention to addresses.

- Invite children to help you name aisles and other passageways in the classroom. Write the "street" names on the board and help children decide on a numbering system. If children sit around tables, a table could be an apartment building, and each child could have an apartment number. Make sure everyone and each area in the room has an address with numbers and street.

- Help children copy their individual addresses on a card. Assign children who write independently to make street markers. Others may make Stop and Yield signs.

- List children's suggestions for a community name on the chalkboard. Conduct a vote to choose a name and place it over the classroom door.

STOP

Visit a Friend

Day 2

 whole class 20 minutes

Materials: none

Review the street names and addresses with the class.

- Ask one child to place something small in his or her right hand to remember right and left. Invite the child to come visit you. Ask the child for his or her address so you can give directions. As you give directions, the child walks the course. For example: "Oh, you live at #6 Main Street. Turn right as you leave your house, and walk to Avenue A (pause for child to follow direction). Walk until you come to #1 Teacher Plaza."

- After the child has reached your desk and returned home, he or she may invite and direct someone to his or her address. Continue until everyone has "visited a friend."

Social Studies Plus!

Making Our Own Map

Day 3

 whole class   15 minutes

Materials: paper, pencils or markers

For this part of the project children should all face the same direction. Allow time to review the street names and some of the addresses.

- Have a volunteer walk from one end of Main Street to the other. Model drawing that street on a map (on the board), label it, and have the children draw and label theirs.

- Finally, model writing the name of your classroom community at the bottom of your map for the children to copy. Collect the maps for use in the next session.

Following the Map

Day 4

 partners   15 minutes

Materials: maps from Day 3

- Have children locate their own addresses on their maps by marking the spot with an "X." Each child should write his or her name and address next to the mark.

- Then pair children so that each child has a partner from another part of the room. Each child should locate the other's address on his or her own map and then trace the route from one address to the other.

Comparing Communities

Day 5

 whole class   15 minutes

Materials: paper, pencils or markers

Ask children to think about how their classroom community is like and different from the community in which they live. Make a chart comparing the two communities. Encourage them to brainstorm ways the communities are alike and different and list them on the chart.

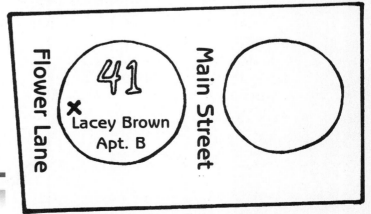

Three House Builders and One Neighborhood Helper

Huffing and puffing is one way to test for better houses. But in this new version of the old story, the three little pigs and the wolf cooperate to show which building materials work best and what laws the community needs.

Session 1: Retell the Story

Ahead of time, have a small group of children color, cut out, and assemble three sets of pig ears and one set of wolf ears from the Pig and Wolf Ears Blackline Master found on page 23.

• Help the children retell "The Three Little Pigs" while volunteers (wearing identifying ears) pantomime the action.

Three pigs go out into the world. Each decides to build a house. The first uses straw, the second, sticks, and the third, bricks. As each house is finished, a hungry wolf appears, and asks each pig to let him in. Of course, the pigs refuse, so the wolf huffs and puffs. First, he blows down the straw house; then, he flattens the stick house (each time, the pigs escape). But no amount of huffing and puffing can blow down the brick house. So the wolf climbs on the roof and drops through the chimney. Bad choice! He lands in a pot of water. That sends the wolf running off, and ends the story.

• Discuss what is alike about each of the pigs' houses and what is different.

Session 2: Testing New Materials

Have the children suppose that the wolf wasn't trying to harm the pigs at all. Suppose that the pigs had asked him to test their houses' strength! Explain that this test helped them build a neighborhood with strong houses.

- Help children think of other strong building materials and then choose three.

- Choose volunteers to pantomime three houses, three pigs, and one wolf. Assign each character a name and house. Give each "house" a sign showing its building material. Prompt actors to mime this story.

Actually, Reddy T. Wolf was just trying to help the pigs find the best material for building houses. This time Izzy A. Pig built a house of (chosen material). Maury D. Pig built a house of (chosen material) and Cyril built one of (chosen material). Reddy T. Wolf, the neighborhood building tester, walked over to Izzy A. Pig's house made of (first choice of material). He huffed and puffed and Izzy's house . . . (pause for suspense) stood! (Repeat for Maury's and Cyril's houses.)

- Ask the class to recall the material that stood up in the original story. Write "brick" on the board and add the three choices that stood up in the new version.

- Have the class participate in a short discussion of how the pigs and wolf cooperated. Explain that the next time the class works on this project it will have to help the wolf and the pigs decide what kind of laws the community needs.

Session 2: Keeping the Community Safe

- First, ask the children to name all the laws (rules) they know about that help keep their community safe and clean. List their choices on the board under the heading "Laws." Guide children to include things such as, stop at stop signs, cross only at crosswalks, put trash in trashcans.

- Have a volunteer act out a scene showing how the pigs or the wolf might obey one of the laws. Have the others guess the law they are obeying. Continue until all of the laws on the list have been dramatized. Announce, "And that is how the story of the three little pigs and the wolf really happened!"

Short-Term Projects

Unit 2

Children learn to recognize north from south when they follow directions to do a special kind of square dance. They also find out that communities come in all shapes and sizes.

A Real SQUARE Dance

 whole class   45 minutes

Materials: directional signs, square dance music (optional)

• Clear a large area in the classroom. Make four large directional signs (NORTH, EAST, SOUTH, and WEST), and post them in the room at eye level of the children.

• Explain that you are going to teach the class a real SQUARE Dance! Tell them that most square dances don't actually make a square, but this one does—because it uses the directions north, east, south, and west. Point out the signs around the room.

• Tell children to follow your directions as you sing. Demonstrate how to "do-si-do" by hooking arms with a child and skipping in a circle. Help children select partners. Do the square dance calls in your best cowhand drawl. Later you may want to add music. Sing (or call) each line slowly the first few times to be sure children follow the lyrics:

> Take four steps north, then do-si-do,
> And four to the east on tippy-toe,
> Go four steps south with your hands in the air,
> Then four to the west, and you've made a square!
>
> (refrain)
>
> North and south, east and west,
> Doing the SQUARE Dance is the best,
> One more time, with all your friends,
> Let's start over and do it again!

• Extend this activity by discussing some local landmarks such as libraries, rivers, lakes, or other cities or towns and by identifying their locations relative to the school. Use four of these familiar landmarks in the blanks of the following stanza:

> Four steps north to _____ we go
> Four steps east to _____, do-si-do.
> Four steps south to _____ now
> Four steps west to _____. Bow!

Now sing the refrain.

Social Studies Plus!

Communities Large and Small   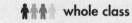 whole class    30 minutes

Materials: books, papers, pencils, crayons or markers

• Lead a class discussion about the community in which your school is located. Obtain as much information as possible from the children. Steer their attention to the size of the community, the size and shapes of buildings, the specific businesses in the community, the kind of housing the children see in the community, special places such as libraries and museums, streets, parks, landmarks, the landscape in and around the community, colors, textures, and smells.

• Using your classroom or school library, help the children find books about communities that are similar to the one where the school is located. Using pictures from the books, conduct a discussion and have the children mention all the things they find that are like their own community.

• List those under the heading Things We Found That Are Like Our Community. At another time have the children find communities that are different from the one where they live and make a list beside the first one, this time heading the column Things We Found That Are Different from Our Community.

• If you wish, children can illustrate items from the lists and display the drawings on a bulletin board under their respective headings.

Remember! Keep working on that Long-Term Project.

Who's got mail? The whole class has mail as children write postcards telling about special things in their community. They also chart change in the community and compose a nonfiction account to document the change.

Special Places in Our Community

- Copy and distribute to children the Postcard Blackline Master (page 24). Explain that they will use these to make postcards that tell something special about their community.

- Ask children to think of places in and around the community that make it special. List their ideas on the board.

- Direct children to choose one place from the list and draw a picture of it on the blank side of the blackline master. Have them write or dictate the name of the place under the picture.

- Show children how to turn the card over, place it in a horizontal or landscape position and draw a line down the center from top to bottom. To the left of the line each child should write or dictate a sentence describing the place they pictured on the other side. Children write or dictate a real or made-up address on the right side of the card.

- If children choose to send to someone in the classroom, they might deliver the postcard to that child's desk or cubby. Other children may want to keep their cards or deliver them to someone at home.

U.S.
Postage

message

address

Groups in Our Community

- Start a word web with "Community Groups" in the center and the names of groups that children identify in your community clustered around it. Examples may include scouting groups, ball teams, after-school groups of all kinds, volunteer or professional firefighter groups and rescue groups, service groups, and patriotic clubs.

- Ask each child to choose one group, write or dictate a sentence that tells something about that group, and draw a picture to illustrate the group.

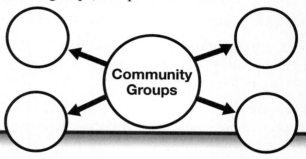

Community Leaders

- On the board, list as many community leaders or leadership positions as the children can name. Prompt them by reading selections from a local newspaper that mentions leaders such as mayor, city council members, police chief, school principal or superintendent, librarian, school board members, outstanding people in business, and so on. Discuss what each one does in the community.

- Then ask the children to choose one leader and write or dictate a one- or two-sentence letter asking that person to come and visit the classroom and provide information about the job that person does. Provide a letter template on the chalkboard for the children to follow.

Changes, Changes

- Display an old photo, drawing, or painting of your school or any public building or public place in the community that the children are familiar with. Allow each child time to examine it. Then ask how many think they know what it is. Focus on the picture, detail by detail, giving clues that eventually reveal its identity.

- Once children recognize what or where it is, encourage them to tell how it is like the present version and how it is different. Make a two-column chart on the board with the headings: How (structure or place) Once Looked, and How (structure or place) Looks Today. Fill the chart as children make observations.

- Have children use the chart to write or dictate a nonfiction description of this change in their community.

Citizenship

Fairness

It's not hard to be fair. Throughout the week, classmates get a chance to show how they can treat each other fairly.

Work with children on understanding the meaning of fairness.

• Give an exaggerated scenario: two friends each paid one dollar for an ice cream cone. One friend got one scoop of ice cream and the other got three scoops. Ask children if they think that is fair. Discuss what makes it unfair. Ask what could make it fair.

• As words such as *equal, same, share,* and *alike* are used, write them on the board and guide children to use similar words in their descriptions of fairness.

• Invite three children to decide and demonstrate a fair way to use a jump rope. Have them tell what made their use of the rope fair. Ask other members of the class if they agree. If they don't, ask a different group to demonstrate a new solution.

• Invite the class to consider other situations at school where fairness is important such as taking turns, sharing materials, and dividing up classroom chores.

• Write children's ideas on chart paper so it can be saved and added to during the week. Tell students to be on the lookout all week for ways they can act fairly toward one another.

• Add children's suggestions to the list throughout the week. Always ask the question "What makes this fair?"

• Finally, have children examine the list and recall one way they showed fairness during the week. Prompt them as necessary: "Oh, Jamal, I noticed that you waited your turn for using the computer yesterday." Or "I saw Jennie and Mia work out a very fair way to share the crayons at the drawing table yesterday."

• Each child can then illustrate his or her own fairness situation and write or dictate a sentence about what made the action fair. Children should share their drawings and their "fairness" statements with the whole class.

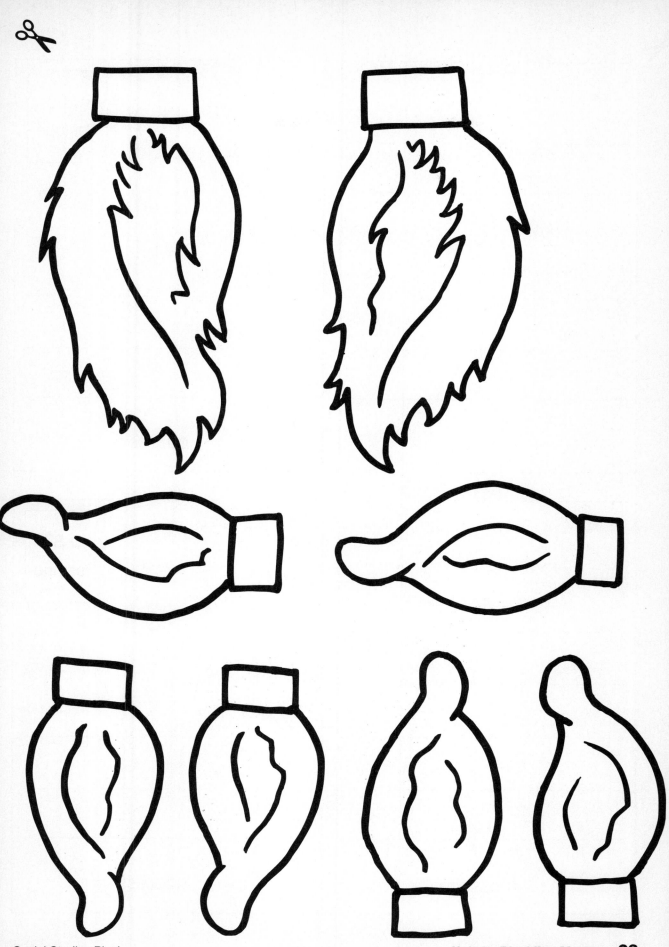

Social Studies Plus!

_____
_____
_____
_____
_____
_____

message

U.S.
Postage

_____
_____

address

_____
_____
_____
_____
_____
_____

message

U.S.
Postage

_____
_____

address

Teacher Planner

Long-Term Project pages 26–27	Materials	🕐	Lesson Link
By Land, By Air, or By Water Students find out how we get goods to people.			Lesson 1
Day 1 👪 **whole class** Students discuss needs and wants.	chart paper, black marker	1 session 15 min.	
Day 2 👪 **whole class** Students begin creating a book about goods.	BLM p. 35, pencils	1 session 25 min.	
Day 3 👪 **whole class** Students discuss the many places goods originate from.	paper, pencils	1 session 20 min.	
Day 4 👪 **whole class** Students complete their books, adding illustrations.	booklets from Day 2, pencils, art materials	1 session 20 min.	
Day 5 👪 **whole class** Students show their books and display them on a bulletin board.	booklets from Day 4	1 session 20 min.	
Unit Drama pages 28–29			
Scenarios: Who, What, Where? 👥 **group** Students chart and role-play different community jobs.	BLM p. 36, pencils	4 sessions 25 min. each	Lesson 4
Short-Term Projects pages 30–31			
Goods and Services 👪 **whole class** Students differentiate between goods and services.	community worker data charts	1 session 20 min.	Lesson 2
A Penny Saved 👪 **whole class** Students figure out how much money they would have if they saved a penny a day.	jar of pennies, envelope, paper, pencils, calendar	1 session 20 min.	Lesson 3
Community Services 👪 **whole class** Students create dioramas to illustrate the types of services available in their community.	shoe boxes, glue, paint, markers, clay	1 session 20 min.	Lesson 4
Toy: From Idea to Store Shelf 👪 **whole class** Students show how a toy was first designed, then produced, and lastly delivered to the toy store.	oaktag, pencils, markers	1 session 20 min.	Lesson 6
Writing Projects pages 32–33			
Chef of the Day 👤 **individual** Students write down recipes and create a class cookbook.	paper, pencils, crayons	1 session 30 min.	Lesson 1
Then and Now 👤 **individual** Students draw "Then and Now" pictures and write descriptions about them.	paper, pencils, crayons, old yearbooks (optional)	1 session 25 min.	Lesson 1
Spending and Saving 👤 **individual** Students write about what they would do with a five dollar bill.	paper, pencils, crayons	1 session 25 min.	Lesson 3
Citizenship Project page 34			
Caring 👪 **whole class** Students design a "We Care at Home" poster showing ways that someone in the family shows caring.	paper, pencils, crayons	1 session 45 min.	Lessons 1–6

Long-Term Project

By Land, By Air, or By Water

**We can grow them. We can make them. People need them.
People want them. What are they? Goods. Find out how we get goods
to those who need or want them.**

Grow It or Make It

Day 1

 whole class   🕐 15 minutes

Materials: chart paper, black marker

Remind children that "goods" are things workers make or grow for
people who need or want them. On a chart write two headings,
"Make," and "Grow." List the children's ideas of things that workers
make and things that workers grow.

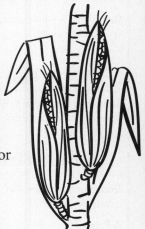

Explain the difference between things people need (nutritious food,
appropriate clothing, and shelter) and things they want but could live
without. Go through each list and discuss needs and wants. Write *N* for
"need" and *W* for "want" after each list item.

What I Grow or Make

Day 2

 whole class   25 minutes

Materials: blackline master (page 35) and pencil

• Tell children that they may choose one of the things from the Make and Grow chart.
Ask a volunteer if his or her choice is made or grown. For goods that are made, discuss
what main materials are needed to make them. For goods that are grown, discuss what
is necessary for growing the goods.

• According to the goods that children choose, assign them job titles such as farmer,
manufacturer, or seamstress. You may want to write these titles on cards for the children.

• Tell the children that each of them will make a book about goods. Distribute copies of
the blackline master on page 35 and help children fold the sheet into fourths to make a
booklet. Tell them that they will be completing only pages 1 and 2 today. Help them fill
in the blanks with words or pictures. Collect for use on Day 3.

How to Get It from Here to There

Day 3

Day 3

 whole class   🕐 20 minutes

Materials: paper and pencil

- Discuss how goods are not always made or grown where they are needed or wanted. Talk about "near" and "far" in terms of your community. You might use a globe or a wall map to demonstrate "near" and "far" in a global way.

- Ask children to suggest ways of getting the fruit to nearby places. Sort their suggestions on a chart under the headings "Land," "Air," and "Water." Ask for ways of getting fruit to faraway places and record those ideas under the same headings.

Transporting Goods

Day 4

 whole class   🕐 20 minutes

Materials: booklets from Day 2, pencils, art materials

- Ask a volunteer to discuss the goods he or she chose to write about in the booklet. Ask if they are made or grown and if people need or want the goods.

- Discuss together how these goods might travel to those who live nearby and to people who live in faraway places. List those suggestions on the board, using the chart.

- Pass out the booklets and help children write or draw on pages three and four.

Sharing What We Learned About Goods

Day 5

 whole class   🕐 20 minutes

Materials: booklets from Day 4

Pass out the booklets from the previous day and celebrate children's work by having volunteers show their drawings and explain to the class about the goods. Display them on a bulletin board, "We Get Goods to Those Who Need and Want Them."

I am a ___farmer___.

I (make/grow) ___apples___.

Who, What, Where?

Players, take your places to demonstrate how community workers use tools to help us meet our needs and wants. Charting the jobs leads to acting out the jobs in a workplace.

Session 1: Charting School Jobs

- Draw a chart on the board like the Community Workers Chart Blackline Master on page 36. Tell children this is a data chart. Under the heading "Workplace," write "School."

- Ask children to decide who works at school, what jobs the people do, and what tool or tools they use. Use the chart to organize and record children's responses. Save the chart.

- Make sure the chart includes principal, teacher, gym teacher, art teacher, librarian, custodian, secretary, and cafeteria worker.

Session 2: Charting Community Workers and Jobs

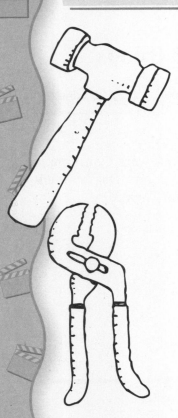

- Ask children to name a workplace they know. Write the workplace on an index card. Solicit at least five different workplaces.

- Tell children that they will work in teams to fill out a chart for one of the workplaces just named. Arrange the class in groups. Give an index card to a child in each group who shares.

- Assign a more independent writer to each group to do as much of the group's recording as he or she can.

- Provide each group with a Community Workers Chart Blackline Master on page 36 and review the entries made on the identical chart on Day 1. Help each group read the name of the workplace and what workers will be at that place.

- Children will take turns recording a worker, the job, and the tools used on their Community Workers Data Chart. Explain that at a later time, each group will act out the jobs on its chart and classmates will try to guess the workers and the workplace.

Session 3: Rehearsal

You may wish to rehearse groups individually as your class schedule allows or have each group work in a different part of the room simultaneously.

- Help each group assign individuals or pairs of children to enact each job on the chart. Explain that they need to use made-up tools and pantomime doing the work.

- Assist those who have difficulty by using exaggerated movements to do some of the things required in your job and asking them to do the same with movements that go with the job they are acting out.

- You may also need to suggest minimal child-made props and signs to make some jobs clear to the observers.

Session 4: Perform for the Class

Allow each group to perform the jobs in its workplace. Ask the audience to raise their hands when they recognize the worker or job. After all the members perform, ask the class for the name of the workplace. Cheer for reluctant performers to encourage all to take part in this dramatization. Encourage additional discussion about the jobs people do, the tools they use, and how these jobs help us meet our needs and wants.

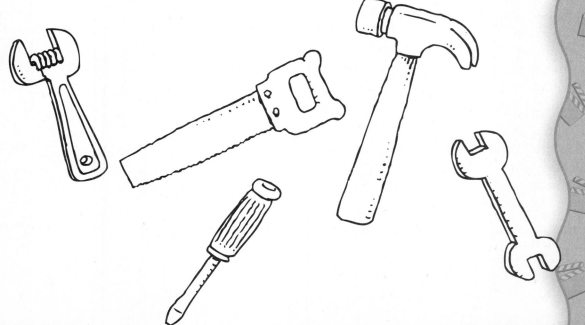

Unit 3 Short-Term Projects

How do new toys come about and how do they get to the stores? What is the difference between goods and services? How much can I save if I save a penny a day? Students ponder these questions while further exploring the world of work.

Toys: From Idea to Store Shelf

 whole class   🕐 20 minutes

Materials: oak tag, pencils, markers

Draw a three-part chart on the chalk board labeled "First," "Next," and "Last." Ask your students to think of a time when they saw a new toy on the store shelf. Explain that many things happened before it got there and that those things had to happen in a certain order.

- <u>First</u>, a designer has an idea and makes drawings or models. Entice your class into brainstorming new ideas for toys. List students' suggestions on the board in the "first" section of the chart.

- <u>Next</u>, the toy is made at a factory, packaged, put in a shipping container, and shipped to a store. List these steps on the chart. Have the class discuss what they know about factories, where they might be, and how some of the toys on their list might get from the factory to a store.

- <u>Last</u>, the toy is put out on a store shelf for people to buy. Talk with the children about how some of the toys on their list might be displayed on a shelf. Review the sequence words and what they mean.

- Show children how to hold drawing paper horizontally and make two folds that create three sections to the paper. Help them copy the labels "First," "Next," and "Last." Then ask children to choose one of the toys on the list or invent a new one. Ask them to draw a picture in each section to show what happened first, next, and last. Children can share results with the class.

- You may wish to staple the papers together with a cover to make a "New Toys: From Idea to You" booklet. Children may also be interested in books from your library on inventors, inventions, how things are made, and how things work.

Social Studies Plus!

Goods and Services

 whole class   20 minutes

Materials: community worker data charts

Show children some of the data charts they made about community workers during Drama. Discuss the differences between "goods" and "services" and how services also fulfill needs or wants. For example, the hair stylist and tour guide provide services to fulfill wants. On the other hand, the police, teachers, caregivers, and doctors fulfill needs. Discuss how some jobs provide both goods and services, like restaurant workers who provide goods—food and services—cooking and serving the food for us. Examine the data charts to see if the community workers are providing goods, services, or both.

Community Services

 whole class   20 minutes

Materials: shoeboxes, glue, paint, markers, clay

Have groups of students create dioramas to illustrate the types of services available in their community. One group may decide to include firefighters, a fire engine, and firehouse in one diorama, for example. Another group may design theirs around a barbershop, complete with chairs, sinks, and customers. Encourage the students to make their creations primarily out of clay, but allow them to also use mixed media (such as paints and markers for the background).

Remember! Keep working on that Long-Term Project.

A Penny Saved

 whole class   20 minutes

Materials: jar of pennies, envelope, paper, pencils, monthly calendar

At a center, provide children with a jar of pennies, an envelope, slips of paper, and a calendar page for the current month. When children go to the center, they are to decide how much they would save by the end of the month if they saved one penny for each remaining day. They should be encouraged to use the pennies from the jar to help them figure it out. Then they write their name, the day's date, and the amount saved using the cent sign on a slip of paper. The slip of paper goes in the envelope for you to check later.

Get your writing tools, we're going to work. From chef to buyer to historian, children learn jobs and make decisions in the workplace.

Spending and Saving

Give children each a play five-dollar bill. Ask them to suppose they just received a gift of five dollars. Ask children to think about things they might buy with five dollars.

• Explain that some workers in the community are buyers. Tell the children that buyers have difficult decisions to make because they have only so much to spend. Ask: *What goods or services could you buy with $5? Could you save part of your money?*

• Ask children to draw pictures of what they might do with their money: buy something to fulfill a need, buy something they want, save it, or some combination of these. Suggest that they write a few sentences at the bottom of the page explaining how they will spend their play money.

• Invite them to share their writing with the class. Suggest they investigate actual prices of the goods or services they have written about to learn if it is possible to purchase these with five dollars.

Chef of the Day

Have available several recipes or a cookbook. Tell children that they are going to learn one of the jobs of a chef. Discuss what a chef does. Tell them that chefs often write down their recipes to share with others. Share examples of recipes, pointing out the section that tells the ingredients and materials needed, and noting the measurement terms. As you read some of the procedures, note words such as *first, next,* and *last.* Discuss how foods are cooked: *cook, bake, boil, simmer, broil, grill,* and *fry.*

• Give children each a sheet of paper and ask them to fold it in half. On the top half, ask them to draw a picture of their favorite food and name these foods.

• Remind the children to think about how a recipe is written, to think of the ingredients, and to think of steps for making their favorite food. Ask them to write these on the bottom half of their paper. Provide an opportunity for sharing. You may want to bind these into a class cookbook.

Then and Now

Find photographs of children in old albums or from school yearbooks dating back as far as possible. This can be even more interesting if children's relatives (mothers, fathers, aunts, or uncles) are in some of the photos.

- Tell the children that they are going to be junior historians. Explain that historians study things that happened in the past to better understand why things are the way they are today.

- Point out photos of children about the same age as those in your class. Promote discussion about details of the clothing the children in the pictures are wearing. Focus on individual items such as shoes, caps, shirts, skirts, and pants. Help children find things in the backgrounds that signify change such as, automobiles, buildings, school desks, and so on.

- Then discuss reasons why children of today might dress differently and why other items in the pictures are different from those of today. Steer children away from, but don't ignore completely, simple change in style and taste. Emphasize the development of stronger and better fabrics and new inventions such as calculators and desktop computers that were not around when the pictures were taken.

- List some of the differences on the chalkboard under the headings of "Then" and "Now" as children's ideas emerge. Examples: Leather shoes, sneakers; dress pants, jeans; dresses or skirts, pants or jeans; pencil and paper, calculator or computer.

- Then have each child draw a "Then and Now" picture and write or dictate one or two sentences about what is the same or different about the "then" part of the picture and the "now" part. Volunteers may display their pictures, read their sentences to the class, and tell why they think the change took place.

Then

Citizenship

Care

Children find out that you don't have to be a grown-up to be a caring person. Children as well can be volunteers.

Write "We Care at School" as the beginning centerpiece of a word web. Use a current newspaper or magazine article about a caring person from your community to remind children what it means to be caring.

- Ask if putting trash in the trash can near the school is a way to show caring for the school. Write "Put trash in trash can," circle it, and connect it to "We Care." Take suggestions from the children and add some of your own until the web has a number of branches.

- Introduce the idea that volunteering to do something to help others without expecting anything in return is a way of caring. Give an adult example such as volunteering at a center that distributes food to homeless people and a child example such as volunteering to help return borrowed books to the school library for the class. Children may offer ideas such as comforting a friend who has been injured or whose feelings have been hurt, keeping classroom supplies where they belong so others can find them, or handling books carefully so others can still use them.

- Distribute paper for children to use to design a "We Care at Home" poster. Each child should think of one way that someone in his or her family shows caring. This can be something the child does, or that a brother or sister, mother or father, or a friend does. The children should illustrate the caring act and write or dictate a caption to complete the poster. The posters can be displayed immediately or saved for a parent's night or for parent-teacher conferences.

Page #3 (inverted):

My _____ are

delivered to nearby

stores by _____.

Page #2 (inverted):

I (make/grow) my _____

from _____.

My Goods

By _____

I am a _____.

I (make/grow) _____

_____.

My goods are delivered
far away by:

_____.

Community Workers Chart

Workplace	Job	Tools

Teacher Planner

Long-Term Project pages 38–39	Materials		Lesson Link
Tremendous Trees. Students discover and celebrate the beauty and importance of trees.			Lesson 1
Day 1 👪 **whole class** Students brainstorm a list of things that come from trees.	chart paper	1 session 20 min.	
Day 2 👪 **whole class** Students create a chart to show how they use things from trees.	word web from Day 1, pencils or crayons, paper	1 session 15 min	
Day 3 👪 **whole class** Students draw a picture of a kind of tree they like.	word web, books about trees, crayons, index cards, sentence strips	1 session 15 min.	
Day 4 👪 **whole class** Students create a banner reading "We Celebrate Trees" and display their tree pictures.	word web, tree charts, tree pictures, sentence strips, banner paper	1 session 15 min.	

Unit Drama pages 40–41			
Scenarios: Weather Dance 👥 **group** Students choreograph dance movements based on the weather.	paper, pencils, instrumental "rain" music	4 sessions 25 min. each	Lesson 2

Short-Term Projects pages 42–43			
Past, Present, Future 👪 **whole class** Students illustrate pictures showing how people produced heat for cooking and warmth in the past, now, and their predictions for the future.	BLM p. 47, pencils or crayons	1 session 20 min.	Lesson 2
Adopt an Endangered Animal 🧍 **individual** Students find out about adopting endangered animals as a class.	drawing paper, crayons or markers, pencils	1 session 20 min.	Lesson 3
Our Land Features 🧍 **individual** Students make recreational posters inviting people to participate in activities related to different land features.	paper, art materials, map of the state	1 session 20 min.	Lesson 4

Writing Projects pages 44–45			
Now and Then 🧍 **individual** Students find pictures of common objects from the past and the present.	paper, pencils, crayons	1 session 25 min.	Lesson 2
Signs for Our Time 🧍 **individual** Students make signs to remind themselves to do their part to reduce, reuse, and recycle.	paper, pencils	1 session 20 min.	Lesson 3
It's All in the Name 🧍 **individual** Students create maps of an imaginary place with a mountain, lake, river, and plain.	paper, pencils, crayons, sample map	1 session 40 min.	Lesson 4

Citizenship Project page 46			
Responsibility 👪 **whole class** Students brainstorm their responsibilities in taking care of their environment.	BLM p. 48, pencils	1 session 45 min.	Lesson 1

Long-Term Project

Tremendous Trees

Trees are one of the Earth's most useful resources. Children will discover and celebrate the beauty and importance of this natural resource.

A Great Resource

Materials: chart paper

• Tell the class that a "natural resource" is something that we use that comes from nature. Then list as many natural resources as the children can furnish. Emphasize that trees are one of Earth's greatest resources.

• Write the word *Trees* as the center of a word web on chart paper. Label one branch "Things That Come from Trees" and subbranches "Things We Use" and "Things We Eat." Label a second branch directly from the center "Ways We Use Trees." Label a third main branch "Ways Birds and Other Animals Use Trees."

• Invite children to suggest items for each category. Write them down and save the web.

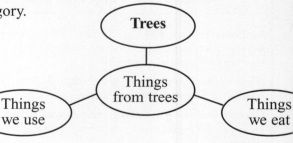

Trees Every Day

Materials: word web from Day 1, pencils or crayons, paper

Revisit the word web, adding new suggestions. Suggest a special event to celebrate trees and all the things they provide.

• Have children create a three-column chart to show how they use things from trees. Fold a sheet of paper into thirds and label them "Before School," "At School," and "After School." Write a title such as "Ways Trees Help Us" at the top.

• Encourage children to use the word web to get ideas to illustrate each time of day. Collect their papers to use at the "Celebrating Trees" event.

Special Trees

Day 3

Materials: word web from Day 1, books about trees, crayons, large index cards, sentence strips

• Check out books about trees from your school library. Invite children to browse for pictures of trees. Tell them to be alert for special trees such as fruit trees and trees with different shapes, branching patterns, and leaves or needles.

• Ask the children to draw and color a picture of one tree they like on a large index card, and then write or dictate a sentence on a strip telling why that tree is special. Collect the pictures and sentence strips and explain that they will use them later to decorate a place in the room to celebrate trees.

Celebrating Trees

Day 4

♦♦♦♦ whole class   🕐 15 minutes

Materials: word web from Day 1, tree charts from Day 2, tree pictures and sentence strips from Day 3, paper for banner

1. To prepare, fasten each of the sentence strips to a tabletop, leaving enough room for children to tape their tree pictures next to their sentence strips.

2. On a bulletin board or wall behind the table, arrange the tree charts the children made under a large banner: "We Celebrate Trees." Exhibit the word web nearby.

3. Distribute the tree pictures from Day 3 and help children cut around their trees leaving an extra inch or so at the bottom of the trunk. Guide them to leave at least an inch of paper on either side of the trunk. Then help them make a fold at the bottom of the trunk to form a tab so the tree can stand up.

4. Help the children tape their trees next to their sentence strips.

5. If possible, invite school staff or parents to share in the tree celebration. Have children tell about the word web, their own tree charts, or their special trees.

Weather Dance

Children explore weather in their region at different times of the year through music and movement. The result is a dance about the weather!

Session 1: Different Kinds of Weather

- Make a chart on the board with three headings: *rainy, sunny,* and *cold*. Ask the class to say words that fit in each group. List the words on the board.

- Explain that they will create dances about the different kinds of weather. Save the lists.

Session 2: A Rainy Day

Choose some instrumental music that sets the mood for "rain" ranging from gentle rain to stormy weather. Then select one or two volunteers to join you in a demonstration.

1. Spread your arms as far as they will reach and turn a full 360 degrees. Make sure your fingers do not touch anyone. Explain that each person has his or her own space.

2. Ask everyone to listen while you play the music. You and each volunteer will choose a word or phrase from the "Rainy" list, listen to the music, and use your bodies to express the chosen word or phrase.

3. Stop the music and see if the other children can guess the word or phrase each of you chose. Children can also explain their movements as they do them.

4. When the process is clear, get all the children on their feet. Have them find their individual spaces and decide what kind of weather or activity they will show. Start the music and let the children improvise.

5. Ask volunteers to perform their improvisations for the class. Have the class discuss the movements and guess what it represents. Focus the discussion on how the weather influences us.

Session 3: Here Comes the Sun

Review with the children the words and phrases listed under "Sunny." Ask them to think about movements that could show the different kinds of sunny weather (warm, hot, *really* hot). Ask them to think about the kinds of things we do on a sunny day.

As in Session 2, have the children define their own "dance spaces" and improvise movements to some music that evokes a sunny day. Repeat the routine of having a group of volunteers perform for the class to guess and discuss.

Session 4: It's Cold Outside!

Select some music that suggests winter weather and winter activities. Review the words and phrases listed under "Cold." Invite the children to choose one of the words listed under "cold" and improvise that word using the routines you developed in Sessions 2 and 3.

If time permits, you may want to divide the children into two groups of "weather" and "activities." Name a season and typical weather, and ask the weather group to dance the weather. Then ask the activities group to act out appropriate activities for that weather. You may want to perform these dances for parents or another class.

Short-Term Projects

People use natural resources to cook their food and stay warm.
Some animals need special consideration to stay alive. Children increase their
awareness of what resources we have and need.

Past, Present, and Future

 whole class · 20 minutes

Materials: Heating and Cooking Blackline Master (page 47), pencils or crayons

Explain that people need to stay warm in cold weather and they need heat to cook their food. Many years ago, the earliest people who lived on Earth burned wood and grass for cooking and warmth.

- Discuss the various natural resources used for heating and cooking today including wood, natural gas, oil, and the sun. Display pictures if they're available.

- Ask children if they know what kinds of natural resources they use at their home. Discuss where the heat comes from in their homes. They may need to ask an adult to show them how their home is heated. Discuss if they cook with electricity, gas, or another fuel.

Give each child a copy of the Heating and Cooking Blackline Master. Tell the children that they can use this to make a three-panel picture about how people have used and may use natural resources to provide heat for cooking and warmth. Ask children to illustrate their pictures showing how people produced heat for cooking and warmth in the past, what we use today, and what they think people might use in the future.

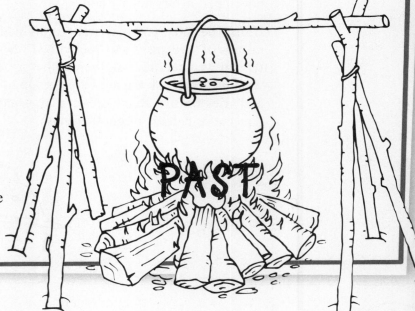

Adopt an Endangered Animal

 individual   ⏱ 20 minutes

Materials: drawing paper, crayons or markers, pencils

Talk with children about the things people and animals need to stay alive (food, water, air, light, and heat). Explain that there are only a few of some animals left. We say they are "endangered," which means that they are in danger of disappearing from Earth entirely. Write "Endangered Animals" on the board and the names of some well-known animals that are currently on the endangered list.

The California condor, blue whale, giant panda, tiger, and mountain gorilla are likely to be on the list. Encourage children to find out as much as they can about one or more of them and then choose one from the list to "adopt." Tell the class that in this case, "adopt" means to find out something that the animal needs and tell others about it. Write the following sentence frame on the board:

"My _____ (animal's name) needs _____ (item it needs) to live."

Have children copy the sentence, fill in the blanks, and illustrate the rest of the page.

Remember!
Keep working
on that
Long-Term Project.

Our Land Features

 individual   ⏱ 20 minutes

Materials: poster-sized sheets of paper, art materials, map of the state

On the map you bring in, ask children what special land features, such as mountains, rivers, lakes, deserts, or forest you have in your community or nearby in your state. Help the children locate these features on the map. List these land features on the board. Ask children to think of special times they have had in or by these land features such as camping, fishing, swimming, and so forth. List the recreational activities that children associate with each special land feature. Divide the children into groups and invite them to make recreational posters inviting people to participate in activities related to each land feature.

Unit 4 Writing Projects

Everyone, and everything, has a history. Children find out that some things were nearly the same in the past as they are now. Other things are very different. Children learn how some places got their names and then make up some place names of their own. Writing reminders to reduce, reuse, and recycle helps keep everyone responsible.

Now and Then

Invite children to name some common objects that many people use every day, such as the telephone, automobile or bus, pencil sharpener, television, toaster, electric mixer, refrigerator, stove, or desk lamp. Each child should choose one of the objects and find a picture of it in an old magazine.

Children can cut out the picture and glue it onto the left half of a sheet of paper or draw the object and write the word *Now* under it. Have them write *Then* on the bottom right of the paper. Children should take their picture home and ask an adult to tell how an item like the one in the picture might have looked long ago. The adult can guide the child's drawing of a "then" picture and help the child write a sentence about what is the same as now and what is different.

Signs for Our Time

Conduct a class discussion about specific things children can do to reduce, reuse, and recycle resources. Distribute two or three half sheets of drawing paper and have children make signs to remind themselves and others how to do their part. Each sign should have one of the three words as a title, for example, "REDUCE—Save water by turning off the faucet while you brush your teeth." Some children will need to dictate their ideas, but others will benefit from your writing words such as "faucet" on the board as the need arises.

It's All in the Name

Review landform words such as *mountain, plain,* and *hill* and kinds of bodies of water such as *lake, river,* and *ocean.* Remind children that when they make a map, they need to create a map key, or set of symbols, to represent the land and water features.

Have children use what they have learned about maps to create a map of an imaginary place with a mountain, a lake, a river, and a plain. Encourage them to make a map key to include each feature on their maps and to label their maps with North, East, South, and West directions.

• Explain that people often name special landforms called landmarks and bodies of water by giving them names based on the way they look. Draw a squiggly line on the board and ask children what they might name a river that looked like the one you drew. Accept reasonable names such as "Snake River," "Squiggle Creek," or "Worm River." Tell children about or show pictures of places such as Bear Mountain, Chimney Rock, Elephant Rock, Rainbow Arch, and the Painted Desert.

• Have children add two or three more places to their maps that reflect special shapes. Hippopotamus Hill, for example, would be in the shape of a hippo and Lake Lizard would have the shape of a lizard. They should write the names next to the shapes. On a separate sheet of paper, children could write directions telling the position of one place on their map in relation to another, for example, "Rainbow Arch is north of Lake Lizard" or "The Painted Desert is west of Tiger Lake."

Responsibility

**Children want to be responsible members of society.
Making Responsibility Diaries will help make them aware
of the ways they can be responsible.**

Each child will need five copies of the Responsibility for Our Resources Diary Blackline Master found on page 48. Write the word *responsibility* on the board. Tell the children that we are all caretakers for our Earth, and that means we have some responsibilities. Ask what responsibilities children have in taking care of Earth.

Guide the discussion to reveal that one of our responsibilities is to care for natural resources by reducing the amount we use, recycling, and reusing some items. Write each word and review the concepts with the children, mentioning that *recycling* means separating items you are throwing away according to the rules in your community; *reducing* means "not using as much," as when you use both sides of a sheet of paper; and *reusing* means using something again, such as washing a plastic cup and using it again. Invite children to mention things they can do for each category.

Guide the class to complete the blackline master. Children should think about the responsibilities they took on today. Some of the students' good deeds may not be appropriate for any of the recycle, reuse, or reduce categories. In that case, children should complete the sentence in the box that begins "I was responsible today when I..." by writing or dictating details about how he or she was responsible.

Pass out a new diary page each day until everyone has completed five pages. Guide the class through the process each day as needed. If time and resources permit, you may want the children to use construction paper to make and decorate covers for their diaries.

Heating and Cooking

Future

Present

Past

Responsibility for Our Resources

Dear Diary,

Today I (circle one or more)

recycled   reduced the amount used   reused

(item) _____ .

I was responsible today when I _____

_____

_____

_____

_____

Teacher Planner

Long-Term Project pages 50–51	Materials	🕐	Lesson Link
Celebrating Our Country's History Students organize a parade featuring people, events, traditions, and symbols of our country.			Lessons 1–3
Day 1 👥 **whole class** Students brainstorm people who helped make our country great.	chart paper	1 session 20 min.	
Day 2 👥 **whole class** Students create signs, banners, and headbands for their parade.	charts from Day 1, oaktag strips, markers, tape	1 session 20 min.	
Day 3 👥 **whole class** Students draw pictures of important figures in American history.	chart pages, various art supplies	1 session 20 min.	
Day 4 👥 **whole class** Students include holidays and important events in their parade.	chart pages, various art supplies	1 session 15 min.	
Day 5 👥 **whole class** Students line up for their parade.	paper clips or tape	1 session 30–45 min.	
Unit Drama pages 52–53			
Scenarios: Thanksgiving for Today 👥 **group** Students write and perform a play based on the values they share with those who sat at the first Thanksgiving.	paper, pencils, BLM p. 59	4 sessions 25–40 min. each	Lesson 5
Short-Term Projects pages 54–55			
Freedom and Choice 👥 **whole class** Students draw pictures of things they have the freedom to choose.	drawing paper, pencils, crayons	1 session 20 min.	Lesson 3
School Symbols 👥 **whole class/individual** 👤 Students brainstorm things that could symbolize their school.	markers*, pencils, paints, paper, clay	1 session 20 min.	Lesson 4
Old Toy to New Toy 👥 **whole class/individual** 👤 Students create inventions for toy wagons in order to make them better.	BLM p. 60, scissors, paste, pencils	1 session 20 min.	Lesson 4
Writing Projects pages 56–57			
More About Life Long Ago 👤 **individual** Students create a K-W-L chart about the many people, places, and events in American history.	paper, pencils, markers*	1 session 30 min.	Lessons 1–2
Freedom Rings 👤 **individual** Students draw diagrams of a symbol of freedom, including a description of why it is important.	paper, pencils, markers*	1 session 20 min.	Lesson 3
Why Vote for Me? 👤 **individual** Students make campaign advertisements.	paper, pencils, markers*	1 session 30 min.	Lesson 6
Citizenship Project pages 58			
Honesty 👥 **whole class** Students make up stories and illustrations showing honesty.	paper, pencils	1 session 45 min.	Lessons 1–6

* or crayons

Unit 5 Long-Term Project

Celebrating Our Country's History

Children celebrate some of the many things that make America interesting and great with a parade featuring people, events, traditions, and symbols of our country.

Looking Forward to Looking Back

Day 1 👫👪 whole class 🕐 20 minutes

Materials: chart paper for the teacher

Introduce the project by telling the class that they will be learning many things about our country that happened long ago and about people who helped make our country great. Explain that you will help children keep track so they can have a big parade later, celebrating the many things they learn.

Write "Things That Happened Long Ago" across the top of one sheet of chart paper and "People" at the top of another. Help children brainstorm things that happened long ago or people who helped make our country great. List all reasonable suggestions.

Starting the Prop Corner

Day 2 👫👪 whole class 🕐 20 minutes

Materials: chart pages from Day 1, oaktag strips about 4" by 24" for each child, markers or crayons, tape or stapler

Help children add new people and events they have learned about to the charts, such as Christopher Columbus and Independence Day. Create categories such as "Holidays" and "Symbols" as children expand their knowledge.

Explain to children that they will need to create signs and banners for their parade. Tell them that today they will make and decorate headbands. Later, they will attach pictures to the headbands that show people and events they want to remember. After you pass out the materials, ask children to suggest colors and designs they might want to use on their headbands. When children have finished, collect the headbands and place them at the "parade prop place."

Some Long Ago Happenings

Day 3

 whole class   🕐 20 minutes

Materials: chart pages from previous days, a variety of drawing and other art materials including half- or quarter-sheets of drawing paper

Quickly review the charts and add and discuss new things the children suggest. Call attention to the "People" list. Distribute drawing paper and supplies. Then ask each child to choose one person or group to draw. Use small pieces of drawing paper so drawings can be attached to each child's headband. Alternatively, children can create a prop that shows something about the person or group. For example, a child who can fold paper to make a boat may make that prop to represent Columbus or his voyage.

History Marches On

Day 4

 whole class   🕐 15 minutes

Materials: chart pages from previous days, a variety of drawing and other art materials including drawing paper

Continue as on Day 3, adding newly learned material to the charts. Children may now have met Benjamin Franklin and been introduced to symbols such as the Liberty Bell. Holidays that may have been introduced include Memorial Day and Martin Luther King Day. Remind children to tell why each new addition is important. During each session leading up to the big parade, children should make one new drawing or prop.

Celebrate!

Day 5

 whole class   🕐 30–45 minutes

Materials: paper clips or tape

- Schedule a rehearsal of the parade in the classroom before the performance.

- On the day of the parade, accompany pairs of children to the "parade prop place," and help them put on their headbands using paper clips or tape. Help arrange their props for use in the parade.

- Line up the children and use music to start the parade.

- At the end, have each child stand next to his or her seat to explain the headband and why the person or event was important.

Thanksgiving for Today

Children recall and retell what they know about the Pilgrims' first Thanksgiving. They write and perform a play, *Act of Kindness*, based on the values they share with the people who sat down together at Plymouth long, long ago.

Session 1: Retelling the Celebration at Plymouth

Help children recall and retell the story of how the Wampanoag (WAHM puh NOH ag) people helped the Pilgrims at Plymouth and how they celebrated a harvest with a day of thanksgiving.

- Invite four or five volunteers to be Pilgrims and four or five more to be Wampanoag to act out the story as you retell it. You may repeat the dramatization so all children can participate.

- Begin a retelling by explaining that the Pilgrims built a village they called Plymouth. Prompt the actors to pantomime each of the actions. Tell how the Native Americans showed the Pilgrims how to grow corn and how to fish. Retell the special day when the Wampanoag and the Pilgrims ate together because they were thankful.

- When the play is over, facilitate a brief class discussion on how the Wampanoag helped the Pilgrims.

Session 2: Long Thanksgiving Dinner

Have children tell some of the ways we celebrate Thanksgiving today, such as having a big dinner at Grandma and Grandpa's house, serving food to elderly or homeless people, and watching the Thanksgiving Day parade. Ask the class to compare these activities to the celebration at Plymouth. Remind the class that there are many newcomers to our country every year.

- Have the children suggest some things people today could do for newcomers to help them get started in this country, such as being friendly and sharing. Write children's suggestions on chart paper.

- Ask how acts of kindness like those suggested might make the newcomers feel. Record the children's responses.

Session 3: Preparing the Script

Call attention to the lists from Day 2.

- Ask children to imagine that a child just moved from a faraway place to their community. Invite each child to create his or her own play called *Act of Kindness* showing how one person can make a newcomer feel welcome.

- Distribute the "Act of Kindness" blackline master on page 59. Explain that each child will choose one act of kindness from the list or invent a new one. Model writing an act of kindness under the title of the play at the top of the paper.

- Guide the class through Scene 1 by writing suggestions on the board that children have about introducing themselves and finding out the newcomers' names. Follow a similar procedure for Scene 2, where the children will write words they will use to show kindness, and for Scene 3, where children write some words the newcomers might use to show how they feel.

Session 4: Performing "Act of Kindness"

Children will all need partners. Each pair should take a few minutes to tell about one another's script and rehearse their parts quietly. Each child will take a turn acting the part of the newcomer. Then have each pair perform its two versions of *Act of Kindness* for the rest of the class. Allow time for audience comments after each performance. You will likely need to set aside more than one time period for these performances in order to give every play thoughtful consideration.

Short-Term Projects

Children complete a diagram of a toy wagon and then add their own "invention" to it. They also explore the many choices that they make every day. Finally, they design symbols for their own school.

Old Toy to New Toy

 whole class/individual 👤   🕐 20 minutes

Materials: blackline master (page 60), scissors, paste or glue, pencils or crayons

- Distribute copies of the blackline master and review what children have learned about diagrams. Then have volunteers tell about the wagon in the picture and experiences they have had with wagons.

- Point out the boxes at the bottom of the page and read the words in each box as children follow. Invite them to notice the four blank boxes, each connected to a different part of the wagon. Have them cut out the boxes at the bottom of the page, find the word that best fits a part of the wagon, and glue that word in the correct blank box. Tell children to save the extra cutout box to use later.

- Invite children to tell what they know about inventors and inventions. If necessary, explain that inventors are people who think up new things to help make life better or easier. Let children mention any inventions or inventors they know about such as Benjamin Franklin.

- Tell them that today they can pretend to be inventors and invent something to add to the wagon that would make it better or more fun. Request children's suggestions, and make a few of your own (headlights, taillights, a siren, a ladder to make it a fire wagon, skis under the wheels to change it into a sled for snowy days). Tell children they should draw their "invention" into the picture. Help them write the word or words for the new part in the cutout blank box, find a good place to attach it, and draw a line from the box to the new part.

       Social Studies Plus!

Freedom and Choice

 whole class 🕐 20 minutes

Materials: drawing paper, pencils and crayons

Help children recall that the Pilgrims wanted their freedom and that freedom includes a person's right to make choices. Invite children to name some things they have freedom to choose. Some may say they get to choose their clothes to wear to school or other places. Some may use a school cafeteria that allows them choices of different foods they can have for lunch. They may be allowed to choose from a selection of books to read or choose a special treat for a special occasion. After a number of suggestions have been made, invite children to select one of their favorite choices and illustrate it. After they have drawn their pictures, they can write or dictate a sentence to tell why freedom to make this choice is important to them.

School Symbols

 whole class/individual 👤 🕐 20 minutes

Materials: markers, pencils, paints, crayons, drawing paper, modeling clay

• Help children recall some symbols of our country and tell what they stand for. Offer important symbols such as the Statue of Liberty, the American flag, the Washington Monument, the Liberty Bell, the bald eagle, the Gateway Arch, and the Alamo if they are not mentioned by the children. Encourage discussion about what each symbol stands for and why that might be important to our country.

• Ask children to think about and tell things that could symbolize their school. Suggestions might include: a statue of a teacher and a child, a flag with a book pictured on it, a statue of a child reading, a sculpture of a large open book, a giant pencil, or a picture of our school building on a flag.

• Then ask each child to design a symbol, draw a picture of it, and write or dictate a sentence telling exactly what the symbol stands for.

• Afterwards have students make their own statue or symbol, using pens, paper, and modeling clay.

Remember! Keep working on that Long-Term Project.

Writing Projects

Children conduct some research, write about their most cherished freedom, and design a campaign poster that announces qualities of good citizenship.

More About Life Long Ago

- Initiate a class discussion about the many people, places, and events children have heard about in studying their country. Then have the class select one person, place, or event that they would like to know more about.

- On chart paper write the selection the class made and under it a K-W-L chart with the headings: *What I Know, What I Want to Know,* and *What I Learned.* Explain each of the three columns. In the *What I Know* column list all the things children say about what they already know.

- In the next column list two or three things the class would like to know. Have each child write or dictate one of the things he or she most wants to find out and draw a picture of the person, place, or event concerned.

- Ask children to suggest some places where they might look or people they might ask to help them find answers. You might want to prompt them by talking about the library or the Internet, or by mentioning a person who could be a resource.

- As answers are found, children can dictate those answers for you to add to the third column of the K-W-L chart. Focus on the answers that were found and how they were found.

Freedom Rings

Encourage children to recall why the Pilgrims came to North America (wanted *freedom* to practice their own religion); why the colonies did not want to be ruled by England (wanted *freedom* to make their own laws); why Dr. Martin Luther King, Jr., worked hard for all Americans to be treated fairly (wanted the same *freedoms* for all Americans); and what the Liberty Bell, the American flag, and the Statue of Liberty stand for (*freedom*). Emphasize the word *freedom* each time it occurs in the discussion and write it on the board.

Invite children to choose one of the symbols of freedom to draw and diagram. Help them write the labels and write or dictate sentences that tell about freedom and why it is so important.

Why Vote for Me?

Check what children know about voting and what it means to vote. Lead a discussion about voting for leaders and for qualities to look for in leaders. On the board, list the citizenship qualities that the children have studied—courage, fairness, caring, respect, responsibility, and honesty.

- Help children recall that one important leader that people vote for in their state is called the governor. Help them remember that the governor works with other leaders to make laws for the state. Invite them to suppose they want people to vote for them as governor of their state.

- Explain that real leaders often use advertisements to tell people why they should vote for them. Suggest that they make their own newspaper ads and, when they are completed, paste them onto actual newspaper pages.

- Distribute a half-sized, or small, sheet of paper to each child. To help them complete their ads, make some of the following suggestions.

  1. Children will need to write their names and the name of their state on their ads.

  2. Remind students of the citizenship qualities that were listed on the board earlier. They may want to use at least two of these qualities to tell people why they would make good governors.

  3. Help children copy any of the words from the board. Encourage them to decorate the citizenship words to make them stand out. Give them some suggestions such as underlining, making bold letters, or using stars around the letters.

  4. Invite children to add more information about themselves if they choose.

- Paste as many ads as will fit onto a sheet of newspaper so that the children will see their work in a different kind of print media.

Unit 5 Citizenship

Honesty

Children consider honesty and explore circumstances where honesty is needed.

Ask a volunteer to remind children of the meaning of *citizen*. If necessary explain that a citizen is a member of a state and country. Prompt children to name the things they have learned about that help make good citizens. Someone may want to recall and retell the story of Eleanor Roosevelt and what made her a good citizen.

- Write the heading "Good citizens are . . ." on the chalkboard and encourage children to contribute their ideas to complete the sentence. They should include words such as *courageous*, *fair*, *caring*, and *responsible*. Introduce the word *honesty* if they do not mention it.

- Invite children to tell what *honesty* means. Their ideas should include telling the truth, being trustworthy, and standing up for what is right, even when others might not agree with you. Invite children to tell why they think honesty is considered an important quality for all citizens.

- Tell a story about Sally who brings a toy along when she goes to Sarah's house to play. When Sally leaves, she is in a hurry and forgets to take the toy with her. Have the children draw a line down the middle of a sheet of drawing paper and then draw a picture on the left side of the page showing the left-behind toy. On the right side have the children draw pictures of what they think Sarah might do with the toy. Encourage children to share the results of their drawing and tell whether Sarah did the honest thing or not.

- You may want to have children make up their own stories and illustrate them in this same way. These should be reviewed with you before they are shared with the whole class.

Name _____   Date _____

Actor's Name ——————————————————————————————

Kindness ——————————————————————————————

Scene 1: Introduction

Scene 2: Kindness

Scene 3: Thanksgiving

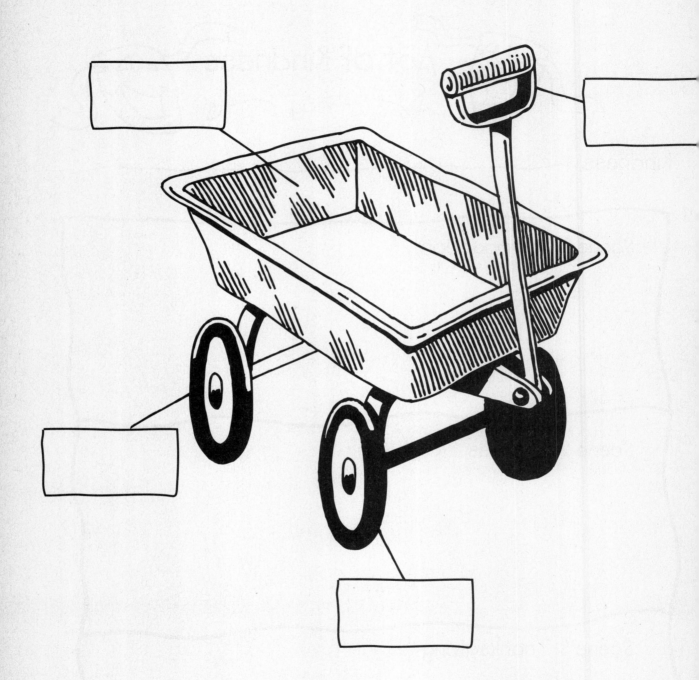

wagon
seat

wheel

wheel

handle

Long-Term Project pages 62–63	Materials	🕐	Lesson Link
Traveling the World Students plan a trip to a place they have heard or read about.			Lessons 1–5
Day 1 🚶🚶🚶 **whole class** Students brainstorm far-off locations that they would like to visit.	classroom map or globe, sticky notes	1 session 15 min.	
Day 2 🚶🚶🚶 **whole class** Students decide where to go and how to get there.	map, BLM p. 71, pencils, crayons	1 session 30 min.	
Day 3 🚶🚶🚶 **whole class** Students look up the foods associated with different places.	postcards, pencils, crayons	1 session 20 min.	
Day 4 🚶🚶🚶 **whole class** Students look up the kinds of homes associated with each place.	postcards, pencils, crayons	1 session 20 min.	

Unit Drama pages 64–65			
Scenarios: Meet the Inventor 🚶🚶 **group** Students act out the parts of different inventors as they learn about the effect their inventions have had on people's lives.	paper, pencils, tape recorder (optional)	3 sessions 25–40 min. each	Lesson 3

Short-Term Projects pages 66–67			
Deciding What to Do 🚶🚶🚶 **whole class** Students review the steps of decision-making.	pencils or crayons	1 session 20 min.	Lesson 1
Changes, Changes 🚶🚶🚶 **whole class** Students draw modern versions of existing inventions.	BLM p. 72, paste, pencils, crayons	1 session 20 min.	Lesson 2
Safety First 🚶🚶🚶 **whole class/individual** 🚶 Students create traffic signals and adapt known playground games using them.	clean milk cartons, drawing paper, crayons	1 session 30 min.	Lesson 4

Writing Projects pages 68–69			
More Than Talk 🚶 **individual** Students draw pictures and write descriptions of them communicating with a far-away pal.	paper, pencils, markers*	1 session 20 min.	Lesson 1
Life in Grandma's Time 🚶 **individual** Students interview a grandparent about changes that have occurred since they were young.	paper, pencils, markers*	1 session 30 min.	Lesson 2
A Song About Travel 🚶🚶🚶 **whole class** Students use familiar tunes to sing songs about different methods of transportation.	paper, pencils, markers*	1 session 25 min.	Lesson 4

Citizenship Project page 70			
Respect 🚶🚶🚶 **whole class** Students discuss ways that they can respect others.	paper, pencils	1 session 45 min.	Lessons 1–5

* or crayons

Long-Term Project

Traveling the World

Children look at places they have read or heard about all over the world and plan a trip. They find that there is a lot to write home about!

Thinking About the World

Day 1

 whole class   15 minutes

Materials: classroom map or globe, sticky notes

To begin you might want to read a book such as *Madeleine in London* or simply show pictures of taxis, busses, boats, and planes.

• Ask children to recall ways they know about for traveling to faraway places. If anyone has visited a far-off place, encourage him or her to share what he or she remembers, especially about food and homes. Point out faraway places children mention on a map or globe, and attach a sticky note with the country or place's name printed on it. Help children focus on how they might travel to some of the places noted.

• Tell children that they will make up a trip to a faraway place. They should think about how to get to this place and how to communicate with others back home while they are on this made-up trip.

Where to Go and How to Get There

Day 2

 whole class   30 minutes

Materials: map or globe from Day 1, "Postcard" blackline master (page 71), pencils and crayons

Review places marked on the globe. Review ways of getting there, and ways travelers can communicate with friends and families while far away. Point out that many travelers stay in touch with postcards. Give each child a copy of the blackline master. Tell them today is the first day of their made-up trip, and time to send the first postcard. Write the date on the board. Help children read and fill in each line. Allow children to dictate their message if necessary. Have them draw themselves on the card front. Help them read the last line together: Wish you were here! Display cards on a "Travel the World" bulletin board, or allow children to deliver them. Help them store Postcards 2 and 3 for the next sessions.

The Food Is Great!

 whole class   20 minutes

Materials: Postcard 2, pencils and crayons

Review the places that children have studied, and have them recall or look up the special food associated with each place. Those who chose other places may need assistance in finding information about food. If possible, help them find out enough to predict what a favorite food might be. If resources are not available, help those children revise the postcard and illustrate something they already know about. When children have completed Postcard 2, either display these cards with Postcard 1 or have children deliver them.

Homes Around the World

 whole class   20 minutes

Materials: Postcard 3, pencils and crayons

Review the places that children have studied and ask them to recall or look up the kind of homes associated with each place. Those who chose other places may need assistance in finding information about homes. If possible, help them find out enough to draw a picture that might represent homes in that place. If resources are not available, then help those children revise the postcard and illustrate something they already know about, perhaps a well-known landmark associated with the place. When children have completed Postcard 3, either display them with the earlier ones or have them delivered.

Children may want to make a homecoming banner, or you could simply offer them a big "Welcome Home."

Meet the Inventor

Children act out the parts of different inventors as they read and learn about the inventions and their effect on people's lives.

Session 1: Meet the Press

You may want to tape-record these sessions or parts of them to be placed at a listening center. They may be used for follow-up discussions about inventors and inventions or shared with parents at a future school event.

Help children recall what an invention is and some inventors they have read and talked about. Focus on a review of Johannes Gutenberg, Alexander Graham Bell, and Thomas Edison and their inventions. Explain that you will be asking volunteers to play the parts of some of these inventors while others in the class will have opportunities to ask the "inventors" questions about their inventions.

Ask the children if they remember how books were made before the invention of the printing press. If necessary, explain that books had to be copied by hand and that it took a very long time to make just one book. Then, Johannes Gutenberg's invention, the printing press, made it possible to print many copies.

Explain to the class that you will be the announcer who introduces Mr. Gutenberg to the audience. You would like a volunteer to play the part of Gutenberg so he can tell the audience what he has invented and how it will help people.

Announce: "Ladies and Gentlemen, I would like you to meet the honorable Johannes Gutenberg and his incredible invention, the printing press. Mr. Gutenberg, will you please tell our audience about your invention and how it will help them?"

After Mr. Gutenberg tells about his invention, the announcer calls on people in the class to ask questions, to tell what they think of his invention, and to tell how they think his invention will help people.

Session 2: Who's Calling?

Review another invention, Alexander Graham Bell's telephone. To set the mood for this invention, play the game Telephone by having children pass a whispered message around the class. Compare the final message with the original message. Did it change? Then have children tell about how they use the telephone and if they think it is important. Choose a volunteer to play Alexander Graham Bell.

Announce: "Ladies and gentlemen, I am honored to introduce you to the inventor of the telephone, Mr. Alexander Graham Bell. He will now tell you something about himself and his wonderful invention."

After Mr. Bell tells about the telephone, the announcer calls on volunteers to ask questions, to tell Mr. Bell what they think of his invention, and to predict how it might help people in the future.

Session 3: Some Bright Ideas

Make the inventor Thomas Edison the subject of another of your announcements.

First review with the class what they have learned about Edison and his inventions, the phonograph and the light bulb. Ask a volunteer to play Edison and prepare the rest of the class to be a responsive audience.

Announce: "Today, my friends, we have the special privilege of meeting an inventor of over 1,000 inventions. But he can speak for himself. Ladies and gentlemen, the one and only Mr. Thomas Alva Edison." Mr. Edison tells the audience about his wonderful phonograph. Your student may need some prompting to help bring out details about the inventions.

The announcer then calls on the audience to respond to Mr. Edison. You can also give Mr. Edison a chance to tell about the light bulb.

As children learn about other inventors and inventions, you may wish to continue this dramatic format to reinforce their learning.

Unit 6 Short-Term Projects

Inventions bring change, such as safer traffic crossings, and more efficient machines. Children consider how things change—and how to make decisions—with these short-term projects.

Safety First

 whole class/individual 🕐 30 minutes

Materials: rinsed juice or milk cartons with tops cut off; drawing paper; red, yellow, and green crayons

Ask children how they think the invention of the car might have changed travel. Then tell your class about an African American inventor, Garrett Morgan, who invented the first electric automatic traffic signal. While other inventors made cars and trains go faster, Mr. Morgan was concerned about traffic jams and the safety of people walking across busy streets. Ask children how they think people controlled traffic before Mr. Morgan's invention. (STOP signs, traffic officers at every corner) Have children tell about traffic lights and how they think they make the streets safer.

Give each child a milk or juice carton with the top cut off. Children can tape or glue drawing paper to the carton and draw three circles on each of the four faces. Model the arrangement on chart paper, calling attention to red at the top, yellow in the middle, and green on the bottom. Children should color a set of three circles on one face of the carton. On the other three faces they should color only one circle on each face—either red at the top, yellow in the middle, or green on the bottom. Discuss the meaning of each color with the words *stop*, *wait*, and *go*. Children may enjoy adapting known playground games or inventing new ones using their "traffic signals."

Social Studies Plus!

Changes, Changes

 whole class 🕐 20 minutes

Materials: copies of the "How Will It Look?" blackline master (page 72), paste, pencils or crayons

- Have children cut out and identify the items from the bottom of the blackline master. Give clues such as: This is what people used for reading at night a long time ago. After all items are identified, ask children to paste them in the Long Ago column. Have children label each object by writing or dictating its name.

- For each object ask children to tell what device we use to do the same job today and how the new version is the same and different from the old one. Then have them draw a picture of a modern version in the Today box.

- Tell children to think of a way to make their object better or more useful in the future. Encourage some whimsy, such as a CD player small enough to fit on your wrist like a watch. Children should illustrate their future version, explain it to the class, and predict how it might change the way people live.

Remember! Keep working on that Long-Term Project.

Deciding What to Do

 whole class 🕐 20 minutes

Materials: pencils or crayons

Suggest that everyone has to make decisions. Ask children to talk about what they get to decide: what after-school activities they go to, or perhaps what kind of pet to have. Tell the class that they will decide what group game to play at recess.

Review the steps that help in making decisions. Write the steps on the blackboard and have an independent reader read them aloud. You can adapt the model below.

1. Tell what decision you need to make: What game shall we play together at recess today?

2. Gather information. Have children suggest different games.

3. List your choices. Children should narrow the choices according to available equipment, school rules, or weather conditions.

4. Discuss what might happen with each choice. Consider whether the games listed can include everyone, and if they can be played within recess time.

5. Make a decision. Help the class reach a consensus decision that is realistic.

You might want to use this as a model for other decisions that your class can make as a group.

Unit 6 Writing Projects

Children write their own songs and take a look at the different ways people communicate. Communicating with elders, they find out how things were long ago.

A Song About Travel

Have children recall a song they all know, such as "Row, Row, Row Your Boat," and sing the first verse together. Remind them that a boat is one kind of transportation, and have a volunteer tell that a boat is used for travel on water. Have children mention some ways to travel by land. Choose one way, and have children substitute words for those in the known song to make a new one for land travel. Using a bicycle, for example, ask: What word could we substitute for *row* if we wanted to write a song about a bicycle?

Children might suggest *pedal*. Write "Pedal, pedal, pedal" on the board and ask: What are we pedaling? Write "your bike." Then read the first line of the song and have the children read it with you. "Pedal, pedal, pedal your bike." Have them guide you to write the next line which might turn out to be, "Bumpily down the road," and the next, which could end up being, "Happily, happily, happily, happily, I think I see a toad."

Having written and read each line together as it was composed, now the class is ready to sing the whole verse together. Children with varying writing abilities may continue at their writing levels. Some may copy the song from the board and decorate the song sheet or illustrate the lyrics. Others may go further, composing new lyrics and writing them on their own. For others, you might write the song on paper at their desks as they watch. Alternatively, a child might rest his or her hand on yours as you write.

More Than Talk

Encourage children to tell about people they speak to each day in school and at home. Then ask how they communicate with people who are far away, such as grandparents, relatives, or friends. Remind children that listening, reading, and writing are also ways to communicate. Have children suggest several ways that people communicate (cards and letters, email, telephone, voice and video recordings, radio, and television).

After a number of ideas have emerged, ask the children to think of one faraway person with whom they would like to communicate. Tell them to think about one thing they would like to say. Next, have each child draw a picture of himself or herself and the other person communicating. The picture might show a grandparent watching a video recording of the child or it could show one child in one house speaking on the telephone to a child in another house. The pictures could also show children writing or having an adult help them write a letter or send an email. Children then write or dictate a sentence about what is happening.

Children could share their pictures by telling the class about them or by displaying them in a communication booklet.

Life in Grandma's Time

Children may enjoy interviewing a grandparent or someone from their grandparent's generation about changes that have occurred since they were six or seven years old.

• Send home a sheet of paper on which children have drawn a vertical line down the center. Children should label the left side "Then" and the right side "Now." After the interview, ask children to draw a picture and write or have an adult help them write a sentence on each side of the line that tells what their elder told them about something that changed. Examples might be the way people washed clothes then and now, the way cars and airplanes have changed, the change from radio to televisions, or from typewriters to computers.

• Invite children to share their pictures and sentences in class.

Unit 6 Citizenship

Respect

Children find that the people they respect most are those who possess other qualities of citizenship—Caring, Responsibility, Fairness, Honesty, and Courage.

Review the definition of *respect* with the class. If children use them, seize on words such as *honor*, *like*, *care for*, and *admire* and introduce similar words to help children understand the concept. Help children remember the story of Joseph Bruchac who had much respect for his elders and for the stories told by Native American elders. Recall that he had so much respect for the stories that he has written some of them down so they can be shared with many people.

- Ask the children to tell about some of the people in their family and community whom they respect. They may think of doctors, nurses, fire fighters, police officers, the mayor, teachers, school janitors, parents, grandparents, classmates, and so on.

- Develop the concept further by asking children to state qualities they think make people worthy of respect. Use questions such as, "What is it that makes you respect Dr. Jones?" Work toward responses that include other traits of good citizenship, such as, "Dr. Jones is honest and helps people," "Mrs. Daly, the art teacher, cares about us and is fair," or, "Mayor Branwin has the courage to stand up for his beliefs."

- Ask children to tell ways people can show that they respect someone. Responses may include, "I can listen when someone speaks to me," "I can be polite to people," and "I can tell them that I appreciate the many ways they help me."

- Have children choose a special person they respect and write or dictate "Dear _____," and a few sentences telling that they respect that person and why. The children may enjoy illustrating their sentences. The "letters" may be displayed on a bulletin board entitled "Respect" or delivered to the person named.

POSTCARD FROM _____

Dear_____ ,

Today is _____ .

I traveled by _____ .

Here is a picture of me arriving.

Wish you were here!

From:

To:

1

POSTCARD FROM _____

Dear_____ ,

Today is _____ ,

and I ate _____ .

It tastes something like _____ .

It looks like this:

Have a great time!

From:

To:

2

POSTCARD FROM _____

Dear_____ ,

Today is _____ .

I saw a home that looks
something like this:

Miss you. See you soon.

From:

To:

3

How Will It Look?

Long Ago	Today	In the Future

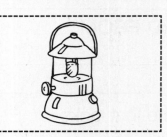

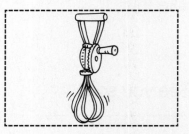

History and Holidays
12 Month Calendar

September *History and Holidays*

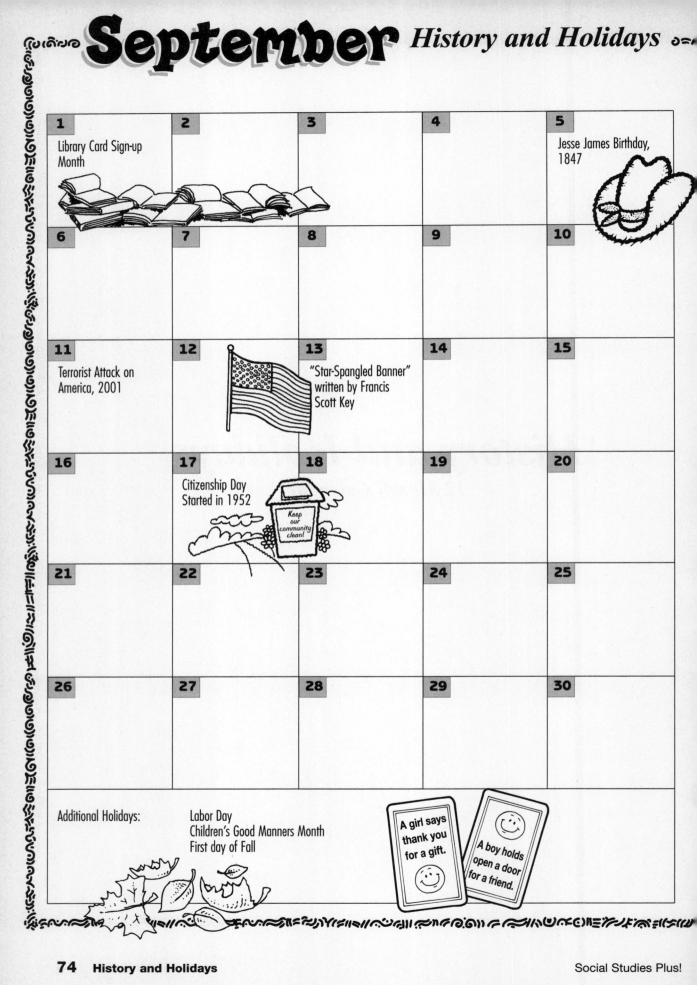

1 Library Card Sign-up Month	**2**	**3**	**4**	**5** Jesse James Birthday, 1847
6	**7**	**8**	**9**	**10**
11 Terrorist Attack on America, 2001	**12**	**13** "Star-Spangled Banner" written by Francis Scott Key	**14**	**15**
16	**17** Citizenship Day Started in 1952	**18**	**19**	**20**
21	**22**	**23**	**24**	**25**
26	**27**	**28**	**29**	**30**

Keep our community clean!

Additional Holidays: Labor Day, Children's Good Manners Month, First day of Fall

A girl says thank you for a gift.

A boy holds open a door for a friend.

October History and Holidays

1	2	3	4	5
6	7	8	9	10
11	12 Columbus Day	13 White House cornerstone laid, 1792	14	15
16 Dictionary Day, Noah Webster Birthday, 1758 World Food Day	17	18	19	20
21	22	23	24 United Nations Day	25
26	27	28 Statue of Liberty Dedication at New York Harbor, 1886	29	30
31 Halloween				

November History and Holidays

1 National Family Literacy Day	**2** Daniel Boone Birthday, 1734	**3** Sandwich Day, Invented by John Montague, 1718	**4**	**5**
6	**7**	**8**	**9**	**10**
11 Veterans Day	**12**	**13**	**14**	**15**
16 United Nations International Day for Tolerance	**17**	**18** Teddy Bear named after Theodore "Teddy" Roosevelt, 1902	**19** Lincoln's Gettysburg Address, 1863	**20** United Nations Universal Children's Day
21	**22**	**23**	**24**	**25** John F. Kennedy Day (Massachusetts)
26 Charles Schulz Birthday, Charlie Brown cartoons Sojourner Truth Death Anniversary, 1883	**27**	**28**	**29**	**30**

Additional Holidays:
National Geography Awareness Week
General Election Day
Thanksgiving Day, 4th Thursday of the month
Macy's Thanksgiving Day Parade

1	2	3	4	5
Rosa Parks Day, anniversary of arrest, 1955				Phillis Wheatley Death Anniversary, 1784
6	7	8	9	10
	National Pearl Harbor Remembrance Day, 1941		Joel Chandler Harris Birthday, 1848, Created the Uncle Remus stories	Human Rights Day
11	12	13	14	15
				Bill of Rights Day
16	17	18	19	20
Boston Tea Party, 1773				
21	22	23	24	25
26	27	28	29	30
		Pledge of Allegiance Recognized, 1945		
31				

Additional Holidays: First day of Winter

January
History and Holidays

1	2	3	4	5
Paul Revere Birthday, 1735 Mummers Parade Betsy Ross Birthday, 1752				George Washington Carver Death Anniversary, 1943

6	7	8	9	10

11	12	13	14	15
				Martin Luther King, Jr. Birthday, 1929

16	17	18	19	20
	Benjamin Franklin Birthday, 1706		Robert E. Lee Birthday, 1807, Confederate leader	

21	22	23	24	25
		School Nurse Day		

26	27	28	29	30
	Lewis Carroll Birthday, 1832, *Alice's Adventures in Wonderland* author			

31

February
History and Holidays

1 Langston Hughes Birthday, 1902	**2** Groundhog Day	**3**	**4** Charles Lindbergh, Birthday, 1902, First to fly solo across the Atlantic	**5**
6 "Babe" Ruth Birthday, 1895	**7**	**8**	**9**	**10**
11	**12** Abraham Lincoln Birthday, 1809	**13**	**14** Valentine's Day	**15**
16	**17**	**18**	**19**	**20**
21	**22** George Washington Birthday, 1732	**23**	**24**	**25**
26	**27**	**28**		

Additional Holidays: Presidents' Day

1	2	3	4	5
6 Michelangelo Birthday, 1475	**7**	**8**	**9**	**10** Harriet Tubman Death Anniversary, 1913, Underground Railroad leader
11	**12**	**13**	**14**	**15** Ides of March (Julius Caesar assassinated, 44 B.C.)
16	**17** Saint Patrick's Day	**18**	**19**	**20**
21	**22**	**23** Liberty Day	**24**	**25**
26	**27**	**28**	**29** Texas Love the Children Day	**30**
31	Additional Holidays:	First day of Spring		

April *History and Holidays*

1 April Fools' Day	**2** Hans Christian Andersen Birthday, 1805 International Children's Book Day	**3**	**4**	**5**
6	**7**	**8**	**9**	**10**
11	**12** Polio Vaccine, 1955, Developed by Dr. Jonas E. Salk	**13** Thomas Jefferson Birthday, 1743	**14** Moment of Laughter Day	**15**
16	**17**	**18** Pet Owners Independence Day Paul Revere's "Midnight Ride," 1775	**19**	**20**
21	**22**	**23**	**24**	**25** Take Our Daughters and Sons To Work Day
26 Arbor Day, National day for planting trees	**27** Ulysses Simpson Grant Birthday, 1822, 18th president	**28**	**29**	**30**

1	2	3	4	5
May Day, Work celebration Law Day	Robert's Rules Day			Cinco De Mayo, Mexico, Anniversary of Battle of Puebla, 1862
6	7	8	9	10
11	12	13	14	15
			Lewis and Clark Expedition, 1804	National Bike to Work Day UN International Day of Families
16	17	18	19	20
21	22	23	24	25
American Red Cross founded, 1881	"Mister Rogers' Neighborhood" TV Premiere, 1967			
26	27	28	29	30
	Rachel Louise Carson Birthday, 1907		John Fitzgerald Kennedy Birthday, 1917, 35th president	
31				

Additional Holidays:

National Family Week, 1st week in May
Mother's Day
National Pet Week, 2nd week in May
Memorial Day, Last Monday in May

June *History and Holidays*

1	**2**	**3**	**4**	**5**
6	**7**	**8**	**9** Donald Duck Birthday, 1934	**10**
11 Jacques Cousteau Birthday, 1910	**12**	**13** 	**14** Flag Day, Proclaimed 1916 Harriet Beecher Stowe Birthday, 1811, *Uncle Tom's Cabin* author	**15**
16	**17**	**18** Dr. Sally Ride, First American woman in space, 1983	**19** Juneteenth, 1868, News of the Emancipation Proclamation reached Texas	**20**
1	**22**	**23**	**24**	**25**
26	**27** "Happy Birthday To You" composed, 1859 Helen Keller Birthday, 1880	**28**	**29**	**30**

Additional Holidays: Father's Day
First day of Summer

July *History and Holidays*

1	2	3	4	5
Battle of Gettysburg, 1863 First U.S. Zoo, 1874			"America the Beautiful" published, 1895 Independence Day, 1776	

6	7	8	9	10

11	12	13	14	15
John Quincy Adams Birthday, 1767, 6th president William Cosby Birthday, 1938			Bastille Day, France, 1789	

16	17	18	19	20
	Opening Day at Disneyland, 1955, Anaheim, CA			

21	22	23	24	25
			Simon Bolivar Birthday, 1783	

26	27	28	29	30
		Parents' Day		

31

August   *History and Holidays*

1	2	3	4	5
				Sisters' Day

6	7	8	9	10
Jamaica Independence Day				

11	12	13	14	15
Frederick Douglass first speaks as a free man, 1841		Annie Oakley Birthday, 1860, Star of Buffalo Bill's Wild West Show		

16	17	18	19	20
	David "Davy" Crockett Birthday, 1786	Virginia Dare Birthday, 1587, First English child born in the New World		

21	22	23	24	25

26	27	28	29	30

31

NOTES

NOTES

NOTES

NOTES

NOTES

NOTES

NOTES

NOTES

NOTES

NOTES

NOTES